First Houses

To Dawn
best wishes

Peter Barkworth

First
Houses

❧❧

Peter Barkworth

Secker & Warburg
London

First published in England 1983 by
Martin Secker & Warburg Limited
54 Poland Street, London W1V 3DF

Copyright © Peter Barkworth 1983

British Library Cataloguing in Publication Data

Barkworth, Peter
  First houses.
  1. Barkworth, Peter   2. Actors—Great Britain
  —Biography
  I. Title
  792'.028'0924   PN2598.B/
  ISBN 0-436-03292-9

Printed and bound in England at
The Pitman Press, Bath

To the memory of my parents, whom I miss.

Contents

Illustrations

Preface

My aim in writing this book is to give as honest an account as I can of my early experiences as an actor in the hope that it will tell young people who want to go on the stage, and those who are at drama school or who have already embarked upon their careers, something about the pitfalls and dangers – and the pleasures too – that they are likely to encounter on their way.

I know everyone's experiences are different, but all actors have a lot in common; and if the book is little more than a comfort to those who find acting exciting but difficult, and whose careers are not *all* plain sailing, it will still have been worthwhile.

The First Time

'Oh I do want to be an actor when I grow up,' I said to my mother when we got home. I don't remember saying it, but she never forgot it and would remind me of it from time to time.

I had been in a play called *Simple Simon*, put on by the 2nd Kenton Wolf-cub pack in our hall next door to the Methodist church at the bottom of the road. It had been written and produced by our leader, Arkela, a small, dumpy woman with a brown face which had a lot of wrinkles in it. She had a quiet voice and smiled a lot, which accounted for the wrinkles round her eyes.

It was just after my fifth birthday and it was my first part in any play. I was Simple Simon, and I wore a white apron over my wolf-cub's uniform, and on my head, instead of my cap with its green segments separated by gold braid, I had a tall white hat with a wider bit at the top, like a chef's.

Of the play itself I can remember nothing; but if I plunge my thoughts back to that winter evening in 1934 I can still recall with the utmost vividness the sheer sensual pleasure I felt from being on a stage. The lights were shining into my eyes and on to my face. The people in the audience were out there somewhere but I couldn't see them because they weren't lit and I was: they were in the darkness and I was in the light. It was my first sight of that great black hole which the auditorium becomes during a performance, and it made me feel powerful and alone. I could sense there were a lot of people there, though, for my voice sounded different: instead of ringing round the hard, bare walls as it had at the rehearsals it was muffled now, absorbed in all the people and their heavy winter clothes. Apparently there wasn't a seat to be had, and some had to stand at the back. I could hear vague audience noises: the rustling of dresses, the creaking of chairs, the occasional nose-blow and cough.

The little play, which was part of a longer evening's entertainment, went as planned and there were no mishaps. The audience was attentive and laughed a bit from time to time. But what was best was the clapping at the end, which got louder as the curtains were opened and quieter every time they closed. Bowing was nice; but even nicer were all the congratulations afterwards. My father put a hand on my shoulder and said, 'Well done, laddie', and my mother said, 'Very good, Peter', and pride shone from her pretty face. Their approbation mattered much more than anybody else's and so it was to continue through my professional life. Part of me always did it for them; and when they died something at the back of me, some safety, some solidity had gone: there seemed less reason for doing it, a diminished purpose . . . and so it continues today.

But then, in 1934, when I had my first taste of their approval, it was glorious. I was completely and utterly happy. There could be no pleasure like it. No wonder I wanted to be an actor when I grew up.

Growing Up

I was in my wolf-cub uniform again the day war was declared. There was a special service at the Methodist church. It started at eleven o'clock so it meant missing hearing Mr Chamberlain on the wireless. The church was full: the grown-ups sat towards the front and the Scouts and Cubs and Guides and Brownies were in rows at the back. The services usually started promptly but this one didn't because, as we later found out, the minister was in a little back room listening to the broadcast so that he could tell us the news. While we waited the organist kept playing very quietly. I looked several times across the aisle at my sister, who was a Brownie; and my mother and father kept turning round to see if we were all right. Everyone was sombre and subdued, expecting the worst.

The minister walked in quite briskly. He was a healthy-looking, bluff man; he wore a gown like a schoolmaster's and had two white tabs sticking out from under his dog-collar. He went straight into the pulpit and the organist stopped playing and turned round anxiously to listen. There was a long pause. 'I'm sorry to have to tell you,' the minister said at last, 'that Mr Chamberlain has just said on the wireless that he has had no reply to his ultimatum to Herr Hitler which expired at eleven o'clock this morning and that therefore this country is at war with Germany.'

Everyone then prayed that the war would be short-lived and that God would show the Germans the error of their ways and get them to see how silly they were not to answer Mr Chamberlain's ultimatum. We sang 'Lead us, Heavenly Father, lead us'; and that morning saw the beginning, for me, of an unflinching conviction that everything We did was right and everything They did was wrong and God was on our side and absolutely not on theirs. The Germans were stupid and beastly and were spoiling everything. After the hymn the air-raid sirens went and my sister started to cry. She scrambled out of her pew and ran down to near the front where my mother and father were. I didn't cry but I decided to join them because secretly I was terribly afraid: I thought that if an air-raid siren sounded it meant a German aeroplane was making straight for us in Kenton with a whole load of bombs which it would drop very accurately wherever the pilot wanted them to go. 'Aren't the Germans awful?' I whispered to my mother as I held her tight, waiting for the bombs to drop all around us and most probably on top of us, killing us all. I couldn't understand how the minister could possibly go on with the service when there was such danger about, but go on with the service he did, though I suspected he put in a few more prayers than he had planned. We prayed and prayed for peace with all our might, while listening out for the dread sound of an enemy aircraft approaching. But none came. And eventually the sirens sounded the all clear. The whole thing, we discovered afterwards, had been a false alarm.

After that everything seemed surprisingly normal. I had expected that all the men would have to go away and fight straight away, that schools would close and shops shut early for lack of food and people to serve it; I had thought no games would be allowed and we would all have to help to make sandbags and air-raid shelters, and live a life of total war.

But not a bit of it. The sirens were silent and the sun shone out of a peaceful September sky. School went on undisturbed, and after school we played hopscotch and marbles and mucking-around-on-bikes as we always had done. I noticed that mother and father seemed a bit subdued and less inclined to play with us than usual: they would talk quietly to each other and stop if we came into the room. They were more inclined to say, 'Less noise, please!' so we would slink off and sit in our separate dens in the garden. These dens were constructed out of clothes-horses, deckchairs and old curtains, and sometimes we called them caravans and pretended we were gipsies. We used to drag mother or father out to them so they could judge which one was best, but we decided not to do this any more. I sat in mine reading *William* books or *The Champion*, and Hazel, my sister, sat in hers, sucking her thumb and twirling the same bit of hair.

Then father started going away for unexplained visits to The North. Since I could remember I had never spent a single night without the whole family being there, and our little suburban semi – three up, two down, bay windows at the front and a couple of Cox's Orange Pippins in the back garden – seemed deserted without him. 'He might have a new job, and that'll mean living somewhere else,' was all mother would tell us. She didn't feel like talking, she said, and would play the piano for hours in the evening. Hazel and I would eventually go up to bed, tired out, and fall asleep listening to Schubert, Chopin or Liszt. She played the piano beautifully: it was her passion, together with bridge in the afternoons and her two children, and it was a great comfort to all of us. 'Mummy's going to play,' would have us scampering in from the garden or the kitchen, though we would sometimes peel away when we'd had enough.

Eventually it was announced: 'Daddy's been promoted. He's going to be sales manager of the Manchester branch of Brown Brothers, the motor trade people: it's a very big branch right in the centre of the city, and the reason Daddy's been away so much is that he's been looking for somewhere for us to live and he's found a house in Bramhall in Cheshire and it sounds very nice. So I'm going to have a look at it now, with Daddy, and you two will stay with Mr and Mrs Hall for a few days while we're away and all being well we'll be moving up there in February.'

I sobbed myself to sleep that night. I didn't want mother to go away, I didn't want to stay with Mr and Mrs Hall, I didn't want Daddy to have a new job, I didn't want to go to mouldy old Manchester and I didn't want to leave Kenton and our little house in Woodgrange Avenue.

But because of the war, and our move up to Bramhall, there began for me such a whirl of activity, I don't know how I crammed it all in. After the bland, effortless days in Kenton when things just happened because they had to, everything now seemed sharper, with clearer demarcations. There was school, of course: nine till four every day and a lot of homework thrown in; there was play with friends in gardens and fields; there were cycle rides through leafy Cheshire lanes and up the high hills of Derbyshire; there was Monopoly and Totopoly and chess and Arthur Ransome books and Hornby trains and Meccano sets and listening to the wireless and playing the piano and going to Sunday School; there was helping in the house, growing vegetables in the garden and queuing at food shops on Saturday mornings. But above all, more and more, dominating everything, there was acting. There were plays on my model theatre, pantomimes at Christmas, elocution lessons, and eventually plays at school, in theatres and on the wireless.

And there were concerts: concerts in people's houses and in church halls and schools and hospitals the length and breadth of Cheshire; concerts to raise money for the War Effort: for local Red Cross societies and Air Training Corps squadrons, for comforts for soldiers and the Local Defence Volunteers. There were special weeks like Salute the Soldier week and Wings for Victory week.

Anyone who could entertain was dragged into these concerts: my
mother played the piano, my sister danced and I hurriedly learned
and wrote as many monologues as I could. Miss Langton, my
elocution teacher, helped me with the pieces. There were serious
poems like 'The Highwayman':

> A highwayman came riding, riding, riding,
> A highwayman came riding,
> Up to the old Inn door . . .

But on the whole I preferred doing funny things and I would go to
French's in Manchester for books like *The Young Reciter's
Repertory* and *Model Music-Hall*, and monologues by John Tilly
and Mabel Constanduros. I loved hearing an audience laugh and
began to think I would probably most like to be a stand-up comic
when I grew up. I developed quite a facility for impersonations
(something I have now lost completely) and did Winston
Churchill, Richard Goolden, Suzette Tarri and Mrs Feather. I did
a funny monologue about a woman playing bridge, called 'Mrs
Tactless Takes a Hand'; during the game I had to look at the cards
in my hand and then say to the other, imaginary, players, 'What a
peculiar face the Queen of Spades has got, hasn't she?' and that
always got a loud laugh. Sometimes I used to dress up in a frock
and wig for this monologue, which strikes me as very odd now but
didn't at all then. Dialects and funny poems made up my not
inconsiderable repertoire. I was quite a success wherever I went,
and my diaries at the time make no effort to conceal this.

Saturday 30 October 1943
. . . after tea we went down to the Victoria Hotel in Bramhall
village to wait for a taxi to take us to Marple where I was
performing in a concert given by the Ladybrook Singers – see
the programme at the end of this diary. The school it was held
in was a big modern elementary senior school. Mummy and I
were taken first to the headmaster's room in which I took off my

coat and tried to tidy my hair, etc. . . . . Then we went into the hall where the concert was to take place: quite a big affair. There was a low stage at one end and on this were several chairs for the chorus. These later entered all in red taffeta (so mummy said). Then, entered the big-wig of the concert, Miss Elsie Harrop. The choir sang without any words or music at all. Mummy says they are the best choral society she has heard – some praise. For the first 'Recital' I gave Mrs Tactless at Bridge and, as encore, 'The King's Breakfast' by A. A. Milne. For the second 'Recital' I gave 'The Old Woman Who Lived in a Shoe'. For an encore some impersonations. Still I had to give something else, they clapped so. I gave 'Little Aggie', a monologue in Lancashire accent. In the interval and afterwards were meals. Terrific congratulations. I think I did my things better than I have ever given them: certainly I enjoyed the concert more than any I have been in.

I can still remember this particular concert well: I can see the large, brightly lit school with its clattery, highly polished wooden floor and stackable chairs. I think what most of all thrilled me was the audience, which was the largest, and therefore the loudest, I had encountered: the laughs came crashing in and I was intoxicated. (It was the loudness of the laughter in *Donkeys' Years*, which I was to be in long afterwards, that kept us going. It was an awkward play to perform but the laughter rewarded us.)

And so I continued my heady way from concert to concert, conscious only of praise and success. Not a cloud of criticism dared to penetrate my ineffably blue horizons. If a newspaper report was damp I would dismiss the writer as 'silly'. If laughs didn't come it was the audience's fault. I expected success and usually got it. Even if I knew things had gone slightly wrong, I assumed no one else would realize: 'The concert,' said another entry in my diary, 'was faulty at beginning and end, but nobody noticed.'

After the concert in Marple my mother became the accompanist of the Ladybrook Singers. When later they joined ENSA and toured far and wide, giving concerts at factories, hospitals and military camps, I would go with them from time to time:

Friday 16 June 1944

Such a crowded day I don't know where to begin. It was the school sports day. I was in the high jump (I was out at 4ft 7ins) and the house relay (which was winning when I was running). Our house, Rowbotham, won the sports. I dashed to Manchester from school, bought myself a book and went for another ENSA concert with the Ladybrook Singers, this time at Baguely Hospital near Altrincham. We entertained wounded soldiers. We had a lovely meal. I went down very well again, and Mr Morehouse, Manager of ENSA up here, congratulated me. When I got home I was at the Tudor Cinema, Bramhall, till after midnight for a rehearsal of the pageant on June 24.

Looking back at my small self from this distance I'm not sure I like him very much: so pleased with himself he seems, so ready for praise and acclamation. But I rather admire him for it, too: he is very honest and when he says people 'clapped so' he says it because they did. He does not feign surprise when a compliment is paid: he expects it. Nor does he make the strenuous efforts most actors do to conceal any conceit or pride in their achievements. (How unlike tennis stars we are, or footballers or boxers or politicians, who never stop boasting in public.) No, he was starting, though he will not have known this, as any performer has to start, on a wave of confidence, and the longer the wave could be sustained at its peak, the better. He was showing off; and that, deep down, is what acting is all about.

*

Quite how I managed to be popular at school I don't know, for I had all the ingredients of an unpopular boy: very good at work, not very good at games – well, hopeless really – hopeless at football which I always tried to avoid, sometimes going to considerable lengths to do so, like pretending I'd got a cough or a really bad headache. I had a secret triumph one day when I told my mother I didn't feel very well. 'You look quite white,' she said, startled and worried, and when she took my temperature it was just above normal, so she put me firmly back to bed for the rest of the day. I knew it was acting, but what a power it gave me, I thought, even over my own body!

My diary kept the secret, just in case: 'Didn't feel well today, so didn't go to school. Stayed in bed.'

I was quite good at athletics, though, and this was something of a redeeming feature; but another unredeeming one was that I had a posh voice: I was from the South and had elocution lessons. Even teachers sometimes took this out on me: I was shocked when Mr Thorpe stopped me while I was reading out loud in his history class and said, in his educated but north-country voice, 'The word is *grass*, Barkworth: *grass*, not grahss.'

I didn't know what to say and can't remember now what I did say, but I knew I couldn't give in to what I thought was wrong, and I displayed a ruthless sticking to my guns which I can still do when I think other people are silly and tell me to do silly things.

However, popular I was. I guess it was partly because I was quite funny – I was as easy to send up as I am now, and was given several nicknames like Beetle or Phyllis – but mostly because I liked acting so much. So, as luck would have it, did a lot of the boys in the class into which I was pitchforked, and from our first term we never stopped concocting concerts and entertainments for the rest of the school.

Luck comes in many strange guises and none has been stranger, for me, than the war and my six years as a pupil at Stockport School. For one thing, it was a comparatively new school; it was opened at Mile End on the Stockport to Buxton road in 1938: a large, rather characterless, bleak building, two storeys high, in yellow brick, four sides round a bare quadrangle. By the time I got there in 1940 there was still no dramatic society: the gap was wide open for me and the boys in my class to fill. And for another thing, the war meant that many of the masters had had to leave and join the forces, and women were enrolled to take their place. We all thought the women were cushier than the men, though we weren't really belligerent towards any of the staff, except poor Skeege, the geography master (but then he was mad), or even towards each other, for the war and our continuing hatred of the Germans and Italians and Japanese was enough. It took all the fight out of us and we were docile and polite and eager to learn, and would have presented a strange contrast to the bullying and unpleasantness that goes on in similar schools today.

The women at Stockport turned up trumps and our greatest stroke of luck was to have Mrs Burn as our English mistress. She had helped us with our early concerts, but she soon had larger ambitions for us. Everyone was crying out for a more serious and scholastic approach to drama than our frivolous concerts provided. In 1944 *Macbeth* was a set book for School Certificate and Mrs Burn decided she would like to direct it with me as Macbeth and Bates as Lady Macbeth.

She was a nervous, highly-strung woman with a funny habit of walking along corridors very close to one wall, touching it as she went. I never saw her in the middle of a corridor. She was pretty, but her eyes were shy, and she had to use every ounce of nervous energy to control the large classes of boys and, now, the even larger cast required by a Shakespeare play. She poured her heart and soul into the rehearsals for *Macbeth*, her thin voice sometimes rising to screaming pitch when she was displeased. She involved the whole school in the play, bringing in the woodwork department to build the scenery, the art department to design and paint it and to do the posters which were put up all over the place, the science department to do the lighting and special effects, and the music department to arrange incidental music.

I felt myself to be very much the centre of all this activity. We started rehearsals in January for the three performances in early April; there was so much to do: not only the play of course, but ordinary school work as well, and we had the most awkward and difficult exams to get through in March. But everybody seemed pleased with the way things were going: the settings were pronounced splendid and the lighting spectacular, clothes were good and lines were learnt and then, wham! bam! just at the last minute I became ill.

My voice went and I was exhausted.

Maybe one of the reasons why actors need so much encouragement to keep their confidence high is that it helps them to be resilient when misfortunes come. And come they do to everyone, and in many different forms. Getting ill at the wrong time is a much dreaded misfortune. It has happened to me at crucial times (at the end of *Donkeys' Years*, when I had to miss my last six performances before handing over to Paul Eddington, and, more recently, at the opening of *A Coat of Varnish* at the Haymarket Theatre). It is debilitating and sapping and no one thanks you for it. No wonder so many actors are hypochondriacs and become experts at remedies and keeping well. They need to. Health foods and vitamin pills, and a lot of exercise of body and voice, are rightly popular.

I managed to get through the performances of *Macbeth*, but it was a terrible strain and struggle and I wasn't nearly as good as I knew I could have been. When the voice goes, everything else seems to go with it and one is left as desolate as Nina in *The*

Seagull: '. . . you can't imagine what it feels like – when you know that you are acting abominably.'

And I had worked so hard:

7 Feb.

After school I was in late detention for half-an-hour (I was late in the morning). Then, with Bates, I had my tea (which I had taken to school) in a room by Mr Cooke's room. Then we went into the office – where there was a fire – and did our homework. At about 7 o'clock we went into the hall and started to rehearse *Macbeth* with Mrs Burn, who was fire-watching. We had chips for supper. I missed the last bus home, and so had to walk the $3\frac{1}{2}$ miles home!!!

8 Mar.

After school there was a rehearsal of *Macbeth*. It is taking shape very well now but it gives me a shock every time I think that we will be giving it for the first night three weeks tomorrow . . .

10 Mar.

The first rehearsal of *Macbeth* with properties and lighting. There is a very clever way of commencing the play: for about $\frac{1}{2}$ a min. before the curtain goes up there are clashes of thunder. The curtain goes up, and the stage is in darkness. Suddenly, there is a flash of lightning with thunder; then the witches appear in a green light.

14 Mar.

After school the tickets for *Macbeth* came out, and I bought 17 for all friends, etc., that want to go. Then there was a rehearsal of Act V. On the way home I took the tickets to most people in their houses.

16 Mar.

My throat was very sore, probably with excessive shouting in *Macbeth*.

17 Mar.

My voice is still horribly hoarse and I can only speak faintly . . .

20 Mar.

After school there was a make-up rehearsal for *Macbeth*. I tried my own beard but the spirit gum simply would NOT fasten it so I had to get Mr Potter to do it. I am doing my own make-up however . . .

27 Mar.

I stayed in bed in the morning, but then got up and went to school after dinner for a dress rehearsal of *Macbeth*. It went very well really, except for one or two technical hitches. It made me and my voice very tired, though, and before I cycled home – it was a gorgeous day – I had a rest and a cup of tea in the office. Unfortunately everybody seems to be getting anxious as to whether I shall be fit for it: I didn't feel too well today.

29 Mar.

Another dress rehearsal. My voice was awful and after Acts I and II I had to stop and did only one more scene: Act V Scene III because of the difficult business with the armour in it (which did not come till yesterday). I had a rest in the office afterwards, and then played the school organ for a time.

30 Mar.

Until 3 o'clock I stayed in bed, trying to sleep as much as possible. Then, after a little tea, I went by bus to school for the first performance of *Macbeth*, when went extremely well – or so says everybody. It started at seven, and although I arrived at school at five I wasn't completely ready till five to seven. Mr and Mrs Couldery were there, and they came round to see me after the show, saying how good they thought it was. I was very hoarse afterwards. I had a taxi home.

31 Mar.

There was a catastrophe tonight: my beard was loose – another sort of gum had been used – and during the famous 'dagger' speech, half my energies were being used in blowing out my moustache. The audience so far have, unfortunately, been of a large school-boy-and-girl proportion, and they have been inclined to laugh in the wrong places.

1 April

Third and last performance of *Macbeth* – I won't say greatest – it was for me the weakest. My voice handicapped me tonight, and in one or two places I seemed to get self-conscious of my lines. When I came to my last line: 'Lay on, Macduff, And damn'd be him that first cries "Hold, enough!"' my voice gave out completely, and I had nothing left but a hoarse whisper.

2 April

I was asleep until about twelve o'clock this morning – after the exertions of these last three nights. I got up for dinner, however, and went to Sunday School with Hazel by bike. Denis Laing and Eric Stennet both said how they had enjoyed *Macbeth* and Joyce Birch (a teacher) said it was excellent. She is an amateur actress. And Mrs Dean said she liked it so much – she has never been to the school before – that she sends by me an anonymous donation of 10 shillings!!! Had a bath.

Not everyone thought it was so good, however, and one of the local papers said, after it had praised several of the other boys, 'The part of Macbeth was played by P. Barkworth, a questionable role for him.'

I tried to think the reporter was silly but it was harder this time.

I was depressed for some time after that.

As a reward for our labours, Mrs Burn took 'all those connected with the play' to the Opera House, Manchester, to see John Gielgud in *Hamlet*. I had read about John Gielgud and had seen some of his more famous photographs, as Trofimov in *The Cherry Orchard*, Hamlet in the 1934 production and Macbeth with his eyebrows meeting in the middle, and I had heard that he was a

Great Actor, but I was quite unprepared for the overwhelming impact his performance was to have on me, for he surpassed all the things of which I thought actors were capable. His voice was more musical than I had imagined possible; I was captivated by his warm, mellow tones, with their touch of vibrato, as soon as he began to speak

> A little more than kin, and less than kind,

and when he became impassioned he never seemed to speak at the top of his voice; it was as though he still had plenty in reserve:

> My fate cries out
> And makes each petty artery in this body
> As hardy as the Nemean lion's nerve.
> Still am I call'd. Unhand me, gentlemen.
> By heaven, I'll make a ghost of him that lets me.
> I say away!

All this in a thrilling crescendo: great crashes like waves breaking. Then, quietly, rapt:

> Go on, I'll follow thee.

He seemed, more than anyone who was with him on the stage, to fill that vast auditorium with pure, liquid notes without apparently making any effort to speak up. He didn't sound loud: he sounded just right for each moment. This knack of easy projection belongs to few actors, though both Frances de la Tour and David de Keyser had it in the marvellous *Duet for One*, recently at the Duke of York's Theatre.

John Gielgud was so passionate and made Hamlet's predicaments so clear that I was moved beyond endurance and had to hide my face with my hands so the other boys wouldn't see I was crying. I was crying with delight, too, with admiration and with wonder that such things as this could be. He cut such a lonely figure and was so obviously distraught, my heart bled for him.

There were other great performances, too, and I remember responding enormously to Miles Malleson's Polonius: he got so worked up when Hamlet was teasing him and he always seemed to be in a frenzy about something. But you knew he was kindness itself and when Hamlet killed him by mistake the whole audience was touched and sorry. Before that we had all laughed a lot at him; but I didn't realize until years later that what Miles Malleson was doing to keep the laughter-temperature high was exaggerating only the emotions of Polonius, and keeping everything else as real as possible. Tony Hancock was to revel in this highly charged comedy-playing later, in *Hancock's Half-Hour*, and in our own time Frankie Howerd does it too, though in a rather different way. Anger (a serious emotion) becomes wrath; worry (also serious) becomes frenzied anxiety. Alec McCowen writes eloquently about the heightened emotions for comedy in his book *Double Bill*. About the National Theatre production of *A Flea in Her Ear* he says, 'I can still vividly recall the amazing tragic frenzy of Geraldine McEwan and Frank Wylie, but there were at least half a dozen performances played with the energy and seriousness demanded of King Lear.' And he says, in another splendid passage, 'To be believable in a ridiculous situation is twice as hard as to be believable in an uncomical situation. The ridiculous situation is nearer the borders of unreality – and if the actor once becomes unreal, the audience and the play are lost.'

It was raining when we came out of the Opera House that Saturday afternoon in 1944. I had not spoken at all since we had left our seats, and couldn't even now while we stood around on the pavement being counted by Mrs Burn. I didn't want to go back to Stockport with the rest of them so I asked her if I could get the Bramhall bus from Lower Moseley Street; she said yes, so I dashed up Peter Street, oblivious of pavements, roads, buildings and people, and thinking of the dream world of theatre and *Hamlet* and John Gielgud and Miles Malleson and Hazel Terry and Leslie Banks and Marian Spencer and all the rest of the cast. The rain was streaming down my face and through my clothes but I did not care; and when I was sitting in the bus, looking out across the dark red streets of Manchester, I knew at last that I didn't want to be a comic or an impersonator or an 'entertainer', I wanted to be a serious and great actor like John Gielgud and attempt as many of the great roles as I could. He had become my idol and guiding star.

My diary is breathless and brief:

15 July 1944
. . . As Hamlet Gielgud was marvellous, absolutely wonderful. I've never seen acting like it, and I learnt more by simply watching him than I ever have done at a lesson . . . It was a magnificent production, lasting nearly 4 hrs. Lovely scenery, lighting and staging. It was really a feast – nothing less (see programme).

I used to stuff the front and back of my diaries with programmes and press cuttings but, alas, they have all disappeared. I think I took them out, intending to make a separate scrapbook of them, and then lost them.

We were less happy when Mrs Burn took us to see an open-air production of *Macbeth*:

. . . went by bus and train to Platt Fields, Man'r, to see *Macbeth*. Ernest Milton, as Macbeth, I (and everyone else from school – it was a school party) thought was awful. He gabbled his lines, said most of them with no expression . . . Vivienne Bennett's Lady Macbeth was, on the other hand, absolutely marvellous . . . See programme.

We all thought Ernest Milton was much better as Leontes in

The Winter's Tale, the other play they presented that summer. And just to set the balance right, I remember being electrified three years later by his hugely eccentric performance in *He Who Gets Slapped* at the Duchess Theatre.

After all this I went to the theatre as often as I could. There was a new repertory company, run by Frank H. Fortescue, at the Hippodrome, Stockport. They did a different play each week, and performed them twice nightly. I saw *The Two Mrs Carrolls*, *The Passing of the Third Floor Back*, *Quiet Wedding* and *When We Are Married*, which my diary says was 'a very hilarious play, with plenty of bad language. Very good. See programme.'

The leading lady of the company was Zelda Davees, a fiery, gutsy actress with a low voice and plenty of passion; her skin was smooth and her smile large and consuming like Edith Evans's and the Queen's. I couldn't believe my eyes when a letter came from her one day, out of the blue, asking if I would be in a play she had written called *For What We Are*. There was a hurried meeting between my father and Frank H. Fortescue, when it was agreed that I should be paid three guineas for the twelve performances, and need rehearse only once, on the Saturday morning before it opened, so I wouldn't have to miss school.

Saturday 22 July 1944

In the morning went for a rehearsal of *For What We Are* at the Hippodrome. I was most surprised I was the only one who knew my lines: the others managed to struggle through some scenes! I suppose it must be an awful strain learning a new part each week, but all the same, considering the play is next week, I should have thought they'd have been further on with it.

But pride came before the inevitable fall, and at the first performance the following Monday the rest of the cast sailed through the play like galleons while I became hesitant and missed an entrance. Things improved after that, though, and we played to packed houses. My diary, as usual, records only the success of the week and totally fails to mention the one incident I can remember now as clearly as if it were yesterday.

I shared a dressing-room with the leading man, whose name was John Hardinge. He was nice and jolly and told dirty stories and on the first night he helped me with my make-up. But later in the week, when I was telling him that oh yes, I did want to be an actor after I left school, he suddenly turned to me and said, 'You'll never be an actor. I would give up the idea now, if I were you. You're just not suited to it . . . you haven't got that basic something which all actors have to have.'

'How can you say that,' I said, nonplussed, but leaping to defend myself, 'when you don't really know me? You've only seen me do this.'

'I can tell,' he said.

'How?' I insisted.

'Because,' he said, 'you don't even know how to stand. You look awkward. And your arms are dreadful. They stick out, instead of hanging naturally by your sides.'

'Well I can alter that, can't I?'

'I don't know. I doubt it.'

I was mortified. And enraged. I hadn't a good word to say about John Hardinge after that. It was a knock, and a serious one, and it sent me reeling.

It took all the pleasure out of acting in that play; and when acting is not a pleasure it is very tedious indeed, and enervating, and dispiriting, and damaging.

Because of the war the BBC Drama Repertory Company had moved up to Manchester – another stroke of luck, for I was to join them for a time whenever they wanted someone for small-boy parts. I had started doing this in 1941 when I was twelve, and was paid a guinea for a Children's Hour play and three guineas for an evening one. I preferred the grown-up, evening plays because they came from the basement of the Central Library which is now the Manchester Library Theatre. It was thought to be safer and quieter there, in case of night-time air raids, than in the high, airy studios of Broadcasting House in Piccadilly. I liked it because it had such a musty atmosphere – so quiet and still, smelling of velvet. We did the plays on the stage, standing around one central microphone. The theatre curtain was always down for the transmission to make the acoustics less echoey, and this increased the claustrophobic, secret feeling. We were so cut off it was hard to believe that people were actually listening to the plays.

I enjoyed broadcasting partly because of the cachet it gave me among my friends, but also because there was plenty of time to talk to the actors and actresses at coffee breaks and tea breaks, and at lunch at Ridgeways or the Kardomah. I loved listening to them talking shop, gossiping about plays and performances and people's private lives. They laughed more than ordinary people, I thought, and were more interesting. They had nice smiles and bright clear voices. They swore occasionally, which I liked (mother and father *never* did), and told rude stories, which I liked even more. I still prefer the company of actors and actresses to anyone else in the world. There is an immediate rapport, a tacit understanding, and they are, to each other, never (well, hardly ever!) boring. I knew I felt strangely at home in their company, more myself, more honest, more open than I did with my parents or even with my friends. I would tell them things I never said at home. With actors anything goes provided you are generous and warm-hearted on and off the stage. There is no need for secrets.

I particularly liked Gladys Young because she seemed interested in me and my life at school. Gladys Spencer was nice too, and Carleton Hobbs and Carl Bernard. I remember being terrifically impressed by Marius Goring, who was Hitler in a very fierce play. He got terribly worked up during the transmission, frothing at the mouth and getting louder and louder, and seemed quite carried away, oblivious of the studio and all the people sitting around watching him. It was the first time I had seen an actor being swept along on an emotional charge like that, and I was as impressed with it then as I have been ever since. Maybe this was because I knew then that I would be incapable of such fervour. This lack of mine was to be a handicap many times in the future. A teacher at RADA, later, wrote in his report: 'All he needs to do now is to apply his knowledge and then "act" with his heart and drive his performances over.'

And years after that I was sitting in a restaurant in Leeds, celebrating the completion of a television play. It was the end of the evening and we'd all had a lot to drink and had drunk it far too quickly. Lally Bowers had also been in the play, and she suddenly turned to me and said, 'You've got a block, here,' and she pointed to my head.

'As a person or as an actor?' my diary records my asking.

Her first answer implied both; then she said, 'As a person.'

'She's right: you should let yourself go more,' said Joan Kemp-Welch, the director, who was sitting on the other side of me. 'You should give more to the other people, especially when you've got the leading part. Give, give, give.'

My diary continues. 'The nicest thing said after the performance was from Joan: "Peter Willes said you could be a real star. And I agree. One more hurdle, the hurdle of freedom of emotion, to cross and you will be."'

That was in 1969, when I was still having to learn that reticence has no part in acting: acting is giving. 'Give, give, give,' said Joan Kemp-Welch. She is a walking example of it, and she's right. Marius Goring had given me my first lesson.

Broadcasting gave me another bad knock, however; I had a part taken away from me on the day of the performance.

It was to have been my first lead in a Children's Hour play and I

My sister Hazel, mother and me in the front garden of our house in Kenton.

Hazel as a Brownie, me as a Wolf-cub.

Me at school.

Macbeth, far left, startled by the rather solid ghost of Banquo (Daniels, centre), with Lady Macbeth (Bates) between us.

Brotherton, Bradshaw, Daniels and me in Caesar and Cleopatra.

As Hamlet, far left.

My parents as I like to remember them.

spent many hours practising it at home. Nan Macdonald, the producer of the programme, had written asking me to suggest two of my friends for crowd parts. I chose Bates from school, and my best friend whose name was John Booth. Unfortunately my voice was beginning to break and was horribly unpredictable. After I had croaked my way through the read-through Nan said, 'I'm sorry, Peter, to do this, but your voice is very husky. Now I'm not taking the part away from you yet, but I'd like to hear David Bates read it.' He read damnably well. 'I think we'd better let David do it,' she said sympathetically, straight away afterwards.

I can't remember what happened after that, except that I was given his crowd part which was on only at the beginning. When I'd done it they said I could go. As I hurried to the station to go back to Lytham St Annes where we were on holiday, I heard the play, and Bates's voice, blaring out from a million wireless sets. I sat in the first empty window-seat I could find, and during the journey stared disconsolately out of the window at the flat Lancashire landscape. Then I got out my diary and wrote in it. I'll get that job done, I thought. The movement of the train jogged my arm and the words went all over the place:

16 June 1943
Poor weather. My most unhappy day of this year so far. Got up at 7.15, had breakfast all to myself, then caught the 8.19 train to Man'r for Children's Hour play *The Ribchester Helmet*. I was going to have the lead. My voice, however, was too heavy, and so Bates had the lead (his 1st broadcast) and I had a chorus part. [Later I added]: After. mummy said Bates sounded as if he was reading it. It was a very poor production.

There were two more productions at school. I have no diary to refer to for either and my memory of them has become hazy, so here is an excerpt from *The Story of Stockport School*, written by

Wilfrid J. Colclough, a ubiquitous and jolly master who taught gym, geography and art.

The Dramatic Society produced . . . two plays in quick succession: in 1945 *Caesar and Cleopatra* by George Bernard Shaw, and in April 1946 Shakespeare's *Hamlet*, in both of which starred Peter Barkworth, who had already asserted his extraordinary talents in former productions . . . In *Hamlet* he was presented with a play and a role most suited to his mature intellect, his intuitive acting ability and his youth. Ably directed by Mrs Mary Burn, Peter Barkworth gave, by any standards, a magnificent performance, and so stimulated the rest of the cast that they too gave to their parts interpretations of the highest order. The inspiration of an 'aristocracy' was nowhere more clearly illustrated than in this production, and fully justified the educational philosophy of those who see in the example and leadership of talented Sixth Formers an influence that enriches the whole. The duel scene with Laertes (Carl P. Bradshaw) was an illustration of this. Neither Barkworth nor Bradshaw knew how to fence, but by a series of carefully and deliberately arranged movements, assiduously rehearsed, both actors produced a simulated and spectacular duel which, when presented to an awed supporting cast, had all the spontaneity and excitement of the sword play of a d'Artagnan or a Rupert of Hentzau. The result was that minor actors were stimulated to efforts well beyond their normal capacity.

A bit over the top, but received with grateful thanks! And I do agree with Colclough's central point that actors are very influenced by whom they are with. Your companions can inspire you to achieve results far beyond those you had anticipated, or they can drag you down. The people you are with in a play matter as much as the play itself.

After *Hamlet* I had decided, finally, that I wanted to be an actor. I did not want to go to university, which my headmaster favoured: I wanted to go to RADA. I learned the audition speeches, which included Orsino's opening speech in *Twelfth Night* and the speech by Tusenbach about looking at a dead tree and foreseeing his own death in *Three Sisters*. I was coached in these by the distinguished teacher Dorothea Alexander who, oh happy chance, was living in Bramhall at the time. I travelled to London twice. The first time for the entrance audition, which I passed, and the second for a scholarship, which I was awarded.

Then came a terrible blow. My father announced he did not think he could afford to keep me in London: the scholarship I had won covered fees only and did not, like other scholarships, carry any contribution towards living expenses. We telephoned Miss Brown, the registrar, to be absolutely sure. 'No,' she confirmed, 'the Michelhill scholarship, which Peter has won, is for fees only; the Leverhulme scholarships and the others which carry living expenses have all been awarded to other new students.'

'Oh dear,' said my father. 'It does make it rather difficult, you see.'

'So sorry,' said Miss Brown.

What was worse, the Michelhill scholarship was for one term only, though it could be followed by a special RADA scholarship with the same conditions, provided I showed exceptional ability in my first term. 'So sorry,' said Miss Brown. 'You'll let us know soon whether Peter intends to take his place here or not, won't you? Because if he doesn't it means that somebody else can.'

'We'll let you know soon,' said my father, and put the telephone down.

It seemed hopeless. We were all mortified and didn't know where to put ourselves. My father explained he was over £3,000 in debt. Half-way through the war he had been ordered to leave Brown Brothers, where he had had a good job, and join, under the Directed Occupations scheme, a wholesale grocers in Stockport as their sales manager. We had one or two perks of oddments of food, which was nice and useful, but his salary was only £8 a week and it had proved insufficient to keep a family of four, with two children at school, even though we lived very frugally and never had any luxuries at all. My father was a Christian Scientist so he neither smoked nor drank. Alcohol, apart from medicinal brandy, in which he had a curious faith and gave to all of us whenever we were off-colour, for whatever reason, was unknown in our house.

I mooched around, sorry for myself, and went for long cycle rides on my own, not wanting to talk to anyone.

Then one morning at six o'clock, when it was still dark outside, there was a quiet tap-tap on my bedroom door. It was my father with his hair tousled and wearing a heavy grey dressing-gown with braid edging. He sat on the edge of my bed. 'I haven't been to bed, laddie,' he said, 'I've been thinking. You've done well and it seems right that you should go to RADA. Well, what I've thought is this: when I smoked and when I drank whisky I reckon it used to cost me about two pounds fifteen shillings a week. Well, if you think you can live on that in London – and I don't know if you can or not – you can have it. Let's call it luxury money.'

'Oh daddy,' I said, '. . . thank you. Oh! Yes I'm sure I could live on it . . . well, I mean, I'll have to, won't I? . . . I'll find some really cheap digs . . .'

'I've been thinking about that, too. We'll get in touch with John Peacock's grandparents . . . they live at Enfield. I'll telephone them and see if you can stay there as a paying guest.'

So it was all arranged. I was to stay in Enfield for 30 shillings a week: full board except for lunches Monday to Friday. That would leave 25 shillings a week for everything else: marvellous! Every Friday afternoon my father went to the Midland Bank in Stockport and paid in the promised £2 15s, and every Monday morning I would go to the Midland Bank near Maples in Tottenham Court Road to draw it out. And this continued for the whole of my two years at RADA.

Sir Kenneth Barnes, then principal of RADA, used to say, 'If they want to act, put them on a stage and let them act. Don't pussyfoot around with too many lessons and theories, just let them get on with it and do it. And do it as much as they can and as often as they can.'

Actors act. Sometimes it's hard to call yourself an actor when you're not acting.

Writers write, painters paint and actors act. And the more they act, the better. Beginnings are so important, and I couldn't complain at all about my childhood. I had been happy, and I had acted my heart out, here, there and everywhere. My parents had been proud of me but had not forced anything upon me, and they gave me a freedom which is more usual today than it was then. And this in spite of so many anxieties of their own. I am always astonished when I think of the love that good parents give to their children. They give so much, and for so long, and expect so little in return. It's the best sort of love there is.

Drama School

I was only just in time. The 629 trolley-bus had crawled its way from Enfield to the terminus just off Tottenham Court Road. A fine thing it'll be if I'm late my first morning, I thought, as I jumped off, tore along University Street and turned right into Gower Street. I couldn't quite remember where RADA was and I started to panic, but then I saw some young people, who looked as if they might be drama students, going into a building just ahead of me on the other side of the street; and, oh yes, there were the two stone figures holding the masks of comedy and tragedy above the door, so that must be it, good, I was there, I had found it; and I was in.

It was dark inside the entrance hall and it took a moment for my eyes to get used to it. There was a babble of excited voices and above them a man was shouting, 'Go to your classes please. Go to your classes. Look at Rainbow Corner to see where you are and then go to your classes. New students to Room 2. New students to Room 2 on the first floor. New st . . . not up that staircase, lad, that's for staff only . . . students use the side staircases to the left and to the right. Hurry on now, it's ten o'clock. New students to Room 2 . . .'

Room 2 was nearly full when I got there, but I saw an empty chair near the front so I excused-me and sorried my way towards it and sat down. Next to me, on my left, was a young man who was so good-looking and so absolutely like an actor, with a pale, smooth skin drawn tightly over noble features, that I felt quite abashed.

'Hello,' he said, welcomingly.

'Hello,' I said, pleased he'd spoken.

'Which class are you in?' he said.

'Oh I don't know yet,' I said, alarmed. Was one supposed to know? 'Do you?'

'Oh yes. But they'll be telling you now. That's what this is for. Miss Brown – that's her – will be telling us about the rules and things and then I believe Sir Kenneth will be coming in.'

Who is this chap who knows such a lot, I thought, feeling even more abashed. I should have done some finding out too.

'My name's John Neville,' he said with a smile, as though he'd known what I was thinking.

'Oh yes,' I said. 'Mine's Peter Barkworth.'

Miss Brown got up to speak. We were all instantly quiet. There was a lot of noise, though, from the traffic in Gower Street outside: someone had opened all the windows because it was a hot morning. 'Oh dear, I think we'd better have those windows closed and will someone open these at the back so we can at least have some air?' She beamed at us. She was tall and thin and wore a black dress with a sort of shawl over it; her hair was done into a bun at the back, but there were a lot of loose bits floating about, and she had a weak chin. Later, when we knew her better, it was generally agreed that she was definitely schoolmarmy and treated us as children rather than as the adults we now were, but that she balanced this by being both efficient and kind and the sort of person you could go to if you were in trouble.

'Thank you *so* much,' she said to the students who had closed and opened the windows, and she beamed again and waited for them to sit down.

'Now dears. First of all I'm going to call the register. Say, "Present" if you are here . . .'

She allocated us to classes – we were divided into three – and told us, as John Neville had said she would, some of the rules and things we needed to know. 'The canteen is on the top floor and the lunches are quite adequate. A full lunch will cost you something in the region of one shilling and ninepence.' I made a quick calculation: eight and ninepence for a week's lunches would leave me sixteen and threepence for travelling, books, theatre visits and coffees. That was all right: I could manage.

She told us, too, about the multi-coloured Rainbow Corner, which had been of her own devising. It was a huge board in the entrance hall, used as a timetable for every class. The different subjects all had their own colour-cards – pink for Acting, yellow for Movement, green for Voice Production and so on – and these were fitted into slots which made it very easy, as she explained, 'to alter the timetable in an emergency. And it gives a splash of colour as one comes into the Academy.' She was obviously very proud of it.

She telephoned down to Sir Kenneth's room to say we were ready. 'So when Sir Kenneth has finished his little talk the first thing you'll all have to do is go down to Rainbow Corner to see what your first lesson is and where it is to be held. Today your first lesson will be at eleven o'clock. Now. Will you all stand?'

Sir Kenneth Barnes came in, asked us to sit, and after welcoming us to RADA and hoping we would have a happy and fulfilling time there, he apologised for the state of the place. 'When you go to the Malet Street classrooms you'll have to pick your way carefully across the bomb site. We have plans to build a new theatre there but of course it won't be completed while you are students of the Academy. But the Little Theatre in the basement is quite adequate.'

He was nice and comforting and fatherly, and we were all

eagerly taking in what we were being told. First days matter, and this was being a good one. When Sir Kenneth had finished we stood up again, and he and Miss Brown left together.

John Neville was not in my class. So I said, 'See you,' and he said, 'Good luck.' I went down to Rainbow Corner to see where I had to be at eleven o'clock: the green card told me it was Voice Production with Clifford Turner in Room 4. And thus my two years at RADA had begun.

My first reaction to my new life in London took me by surprise, though I suppose it ought not to have done. I should have expected it, but I hadn't: I was free.

I was on my own. I could do as I liked. Of course, there was 10 to 5.30 at RADA, but afterwards free evenings and free weekends. I didn't have to account for everything I did or answer the dreaded question: 'What did you do today?' I could walk the streets, go to the theatre or the cinema or out into the country without having to *say* what I was going to do. I didn't have to be back at any particular time and I could go to bed when I liked. I could sit in cafés, usually Olivelli's in Store Street or Taylor's in Tottenham Court Road, and talk into the night with my new friends. Again I loved the gossip and the openness: the feeling that anything goes provided you're nice and kind. There were no dogmatic rights and wrongs to be considered.

But not only was I free, I was free in London. The war was over and it was a safe place once more and I knew it was there I wanted to be. The cafés and the restaurants (Lyon's Corner Houses, and Schmidt's in Charlotte Street for special treats), Foyles for books and Marks & Spencers for clothes, the warm smell from the entrances to Underground stations and the look of the city from the path across Hungerford Bridge; these and many other things intoxicated me. And cinemas and theatres, of course. I lived at last in the metropolis, in the centre of the entertainment industry. (It's easier for actors in England, with everything centred on London, than for Americans with their film and television studios in Los Angeles being so far from the theatres in New York.)

I went to the theatre about once a week and sat in the gallery for sixpence or a shilling, pondering over the finer points of the performances. 'Oh that's good,' I remember saying to a friend one evening, 'she lifts her head from time to time so that we up here can see her face. The others don't and they seem further away.'

'Yes it is good,' said my friend. 'The others have forgotten the gods. We must remember them.'

The great seasons presented by the Old Vic Company at the New Theatre (now the Albery) coincided with my time at RADA, and we were able to see Laurence Olivier, Ralph Richardson, Margaret Leighton, Joyce Redman, Harry Andrews and Alec Guinness all at the peak of their form in remarkable productions of *Richard the Third*, *Cyrano de Bergerac*, *An Inspector Calls*, *Arms and the Man* and many other plays. What a splendid, unsurpassed time that was! How we chattered about the acting, dissecting it, often surprisingly critically! 'Do you prefer Gielgud or Olivier?' was the stock question, over which we were prepared to debate for hours. 'What do you think of Richardson?' was another which invited prolonged discussion.

Freedom and living in London were the blissful bonuses of being at a drama school. But more important to me than the freedom and even more than being in London was that I was now in the company of young people who lived, breathed and dreamed theatre as much as I did. No longer did I stand out in the crowd; there were some here who were better than I was and I knew I had my work cut out. Competition was rife and we were a critical lot.

In my class there were two boys who were to influence me a great deal: Strowan Robertson and Robert Shaw. Strowan was a floppy Canadian who was not much of an actor; but we all thought he was something of an intellectual because he wrote poetry and knew about literature. He had a loud laugh and was full of jokes and enjoyed talking about acting; and as he seemed to enjoy talking about *my* acting I relied on his friendship: he was the first person I had met to whom I could talk myself out. We had hours and hours of coffees in late-night bistros.

I didn't like Robert at all at first. I thought he was arrogant and boastful and too like a peacock: he paraded himself in front of us and swaggered. I didn't think he was very good, either: stiff and stylized and with a boring voice.

The dislike was reciprocated, I was sure of it. He was sneering and uncommunicative. We were not so much enemies as rivals and we divided the class, for a time, into the Shaw camp and the Barkworth camp. But one evening in our second term we were the last to leave a class. In a very off-hand way he said he was going to see a film and would I like to come too. I was horrified. The idea of an evening alone with Robert was appalling. He would just attack me and say how weak I was and go on sneering at me. But I didn't have any plans for the evening and couldn't think of an excuse quickly enough so I said yes I would.

We saw *Les Enfants du Paradis* at the Academy Cinema in Oxford Street and afterwards had coffees and cakes in a nearby café. We had been very moved by the film and talked well about it. Then we got on to shop-talk and gossip, and we went through all our class-mates and discovered we were in total agreement about them. We progressed to the more dangerous subject of ourselves, concentrating, naturally, on what we could find to admire in each other. To our mutual surprise we found quite a lot. I was amazed to hear myself praising him for his authority, his intelligence, his daring, dash and moments of bravura. He praised me too (I forget what for), and we realized we had far more in common than we had hitherto suspected. From that evening we were the firmest of friends and astounded the class next day by going around together and being as nice as pie about each other.

Strowan had a basement flat in Regent's Park Road, facing Primrose Hill, but he wanted to leave it and move to South Kensington on account of some poets he knew there. 'As you two are now living in each other's pockets,' he said sarcastically, 'why don't you share it? You could have a room each and it's only three pounds a week.' We thought it was a good idea and could both just afford it. Robert was as hard up as I was, but we agreed that if we shopped at the market in Camden Town and ate at home whenever we could we would save on cafés and restaurants and thus be able to make ends meet.

For some months it all worked out splendidly and we helped and hindered each other in about equal proportions. He was very stimulating and started to write a lot of poetry. My most recurring picture is of him lying on his stomach on the slopes of Primrose Hill, scribbling away, oblivious of everything except what he was inventing in the deep parts of his mind. I would sit there, watching him, pretending to read a book or learn some lines; and when I was tired of that I would close my eyes and lie back and bask in the hot summer sun.

Later our differences and rivalry reasserted themselves, and I decided to move out and live in more docile surroundings in a rooming house in Dulwich. But secretly I was never as happy there, or as excited, as I had been in our flat in Regent's Park Road. I still have a soft spot for that part of London, with the peace of Primrose Hill and the park so near to the noisy bustle of Camden Town. Now I live in Hampstead, which is not too far away.

Although we drifted apart when we finished at RADA and saw each other only once or twice, I was appalled by his early death. He was a great striver and was only happy when he was winning. His energy and power were, to me, colossal, and I couldn't keep up with him; but I wouldn't have missed those months of close friendship for anything.

On the whole, we thought, the teachers were good. Some were too gentle and easily pleased, and at least one was too fierce and made people cry or get angry, according to their nature; but no, on the whole, they were good. Best were Fabia Drake and Clifford Turner. Hugh Miller was fine, but he remained something of a remote figure himself so his Technique classes didn't have the entertainment value of Fabia's. He was more interested in the subject, which he adored, than in us, which left us feeling curiously inadequate and out of things. Mary Phillips, who did Mime, and Amy Boalth, who did Movement, were nice and clever; but Mime was not anybody's favourite so we weren't very good at it, and Movement seemed to have little connection with the sort of walking about you have to do in plays, being more concerned with expression to music, so we regarded the classes as a rest from the serious business of acting and enjoyed them accordingly. We wore black tights for Movement and swanned about expressively, doing big gestures to please Miss Boalth, who coaxed us in her clattering voice to 'Rise up to Heaven – two – three – four, sink down to earth – two – three – four,' while the kindly lady pianist tinkled on, expressively but out of tune.

Fabia Drake's Technique classes were brilliant. She was big and dominating and had a swoopy voice, but we all agreed she knew her stuff. I remember two of her exercises vividly and cribbed them for my classes when I became a teacher. One was: we had to find a dull passage to read, and make it interesting by using as much variety as we could and injecting attractive qualities like romance, charm or drama. I think I remember this exercise clearly because it was one of my few triumphs in Fabia's classes:

'Now Peter Barkworth. Your turn. What have you chosen?'

'A bit from the Bible, Miss Drake,' I said nervously as I got up.

'No, sit down Peter. That won't do. I said a dull passage, and you've chosen something from one of the greatest works of literature. The Bible is beautiful. Beautiful,' she swooned; and she looked around the class for slight nods of wise agreement that of course the Bible was beautiful and could not possibly qualify for this exercise. The others had all chosen from the telephone directory or the index at the back of a book.

'No Miss Drake,' I said, still standing, 'I promise you this is dull.'

'Which book of the Bible is it from?'

'St Matthew.'

'St *Matthew*?' she cried, sounding even more like Lady Bracknell. And then suddenly, and cross: 'Sit down.'

'No Miss Drake it *is* dull,' I implored. 'It's that bit about people begetting each other.'

'Well,' she relented, 'go on. Do it.'

So I started: 'Abraham begat Isaac; and Isaac begat Jacob; and Jacob begat Judas and his brethren; and Judas begat Phares and Zara of Thamar'; and a hush fell in the classroom: I was seeing those people with their strange-sounding names, and made the most of every opportunity for variety like Judas *and his brethren*, and Phares *and* Zara. Then I did a bit quickly, giving a feeling of the succession of births: 'And Aram begat Aminadab; and Aminadab begat Naasson; and Naasson begat Salmon . . .' Then I did a bit as though it was really leading up to something big, and it was! 'And Booz begat Obed of Ruth; and Obed begat Jesse; and Jesse begat [*slight pause: wait for it*] David [*another slight pause, then romantic and hushed*] the king.' You could have heard a pin drop. A long pause. Then, quietly and slowly: 'And David the king begat Solomon [*dwell on that name*] of her that *had* been [*mystery here*] the wife of Urias [*what went wrong with that marriage?*].'

I managed a few more begats and then burst out giggling. The suspense was too much and more than I'd bargained for.

'Oh Peter,' said Fabia, 'you've spoiled it. Sit down. But until you laughed, which was a very stupid thing to do, it was good. Very good. You seized every opportunity. Didn't he?'

'Yes,' chorused the class.

'We all know how he did it, don't we?'

'Yes,' repeated the class, obediently.

'Splendid, Peter, splendid. Next?'

Oh, there's no feeling like it in the world, knowing you've done good work, and knowing everyone else thinks so too. I thought of this exercise again the other day when I went to a performance of St Mark's Gospel – Alec McCowen's extraordinary penetration into the meaning and drama of the story of Jesus.

'And there were also with him other – *little* – ships . . . And he arose, and rebuked the wind, and said unto the sea, Peace, be still. And the wind ceased, and [*hushed, slow, full of wonder*] there was a great calm.'

It was an astonishing performance, full of energy, immediacy and surprises.

'And they that went before, and they that followed, cried, saying [*this loud and energetic; then straight away, but soft and swaying, with high wafting gestures, as though waving sticks of palm*], Hosanna; Blessed is he that cometh in the name of the Lord.'

Alec McCowen's mastery of the craft of acting is an object lesson: his choices are impeccable and his presentation beyond reproach.

The other exercise of Fabia's I liked so much was to do 'Speak the speech I pray you . . .' from *Hamlet*, with five gestures. 'Not four, not six. Five. Five good, illuminating, well executed gestures. And when you are not gesturing, your hands should be properly at rest.' It's a fine exercise, this, teaching control over arms and hands. And I like the mathematical exactness of it: five, not four, not six. I found myself saying the other day to a friend who was starting work on a part he thought was going to prove a bit awkward: 'Well, I think you could set yourself the task with this part of finding, say, three clear differences between yourself and the character. Three clear habits, or mannerisms, which will illuminate the character and his state of mind . . . they can be mannerisms of speech, or walking, or standing, or anything. If possible let them be things you have never used before.' I have always particularly liked sonnets, with their fourteen lines ending with a couplet, or limericks, with three long lines and two short ones in the middle. Strictness and rules can often bring surprisingly free results.

Clifford Turner had a lot of strictness and rules for us in his Voice Production classes, the main one being that we should use a method of breathing called 'rib reserve breathing'. 'Rib resahve breathing,' I can hear him saying, in his sonorous baritone. We all agreed that Clifford Turner's voice was too perfect for him ever to be an actor, but because we could never achieve a similar perfection, it was all right to follow his methods. The goal he set us was unattainable, thank goodness, though it did us no harm to strive a little way towards it.

When he demonstrated rib reserve breathing, he stood with one hand on his hip, and the other pointing inwards with the fingertips touching his diaphragm. He filled his lungs with air, noisily, to demonstrate. 'Now,' he intoned, giving a commentary, 'my rib-cage is expanded and my lungs are full of air. That is the breath which I keep in resahve, and I breathe in and out with my diaphragm only.' And he demonstrated. 'Breathe in . . .' and the fingers touching his diaphragm were pushed out alarmingly, 'breathe out . . .' and they went back to where they were. 'Breathe in . . .' he continued, 'breathe out . . .' We thought he would expire. 'Rib resahve breathing,' he concluded, 'very good for breath control, even bettah for resonance.'

He was tall and gaunt and good-looking and we all loved him. He was a lonely man, I later discovered, but there was no sign of that in the classroom. His delight when he saw any signs of improvement made us laugh with pleasure. 'Bettah, bettah,' he would say, and we would laugh even more, for we used to imitate him behind his back and 'Bettah, bettah' had become a catch-phrase. That, and his laugh, a slow 'Hah, hah, hah', very low.

He had what all good teachers have: a thorough knowledge of their subject, an ability to convey that knowledge in an entertaining way, and a love of other people. Teachers must be generous; it's hopeless when they are not.

I was enjoying myself and was held in some regard, I think; and at the end of my first term I was awarded the RADA scholarship I had hoped for. My mother and father were overjoyed at this news when I told them about it at Christmas, for it meant I could finish the course. I flourished my report and got them to read it. 'You have shown decided promise and keenness, a real sense of character and dramatic expression,' said Sir Kenneth. Clifford Turner said I was a keen student, too, but that I was 'inclined to be too precise'.

My father asked if I was managing on the £2 15s a week he was sending me and I said, 'Oh yes', which was true, and he beamed. Only later did I learn how desperately difficult it had been for him to keep it up: immediately after the war he had resigned from the wholesale grocers to set up on his own as a manufacturer's agent. Getting going was a slow process and he made little money to start with.

I was very garrulous about RADA that Christmas, and very happy. Mother and father were pleased I was so talkative, for during my last months at school I had become reserved and uncommunicative, resenting their perpetual inquiries. 'RADA is obviously doing you good,' said my mother.

'Oh yes,' I said, 'and everybody says it's a very good time to be there because there's such a wide range of ages; a lot of them were in the forces during the war and some of them are really old: there's a boy in my class – well, man really – who's twenty-seven! But at any rate it means there are lots of people to play mothers and fathers and the older parts.'

'And you don't mind being in London and away from home?' asked my father.

'Oh no, I love it,' I said, rather too quickly.

A silence fell.

'Good,' he said, eventually.

The other evening, at sunset, I went for a stroll around the streets near RADA. How unchanged they are! Olivelli's is a hotel now instead of a café and Taylor's is an amusement arcade. But it all has the same discreet, bookish, Bloomsbury look, and the pubs have the same names and were just as brimful of students as they used to be: the Rising Sun in Tottenham Court Road, the University Tavern in Store Street and the Marlborough Arms in Torrington Place. I went into the University Tavern, where some RADA students were sitting round a table drinking and laughing, talking loudly and showing off. I was transported back. It was as though it were yesterday. I wanted to join them, but I looked away: they reminded me too painfully of Robert and Strowan, Clare and Diana, Leora and Ruth. Where are they now, those that I knew so well and have not heard of from that day to this? So many of them gave up and disappeared. Some did very well, like Robert, and John Neville and Theodore Bickel and Peter Sallis and Barbara Jefford and Laurence Harvey and Fulton McKay and Brian Wilde and Robert Urquhart and Harold Goodwin and Adrienne Corri and Brewster Mason; others have had distinguished careers in other fields, like James Gilbert, the BBC Light Entertainment producer, and Michael Anderson, a top agent. And some have died. But where, I wonder, are all the others? What are they doing now?

I didn't keep a day-to-day diary when I was a RADA student. All I have now are a few notebooks, my reports, and a 'journal' in which I wrote at length from time to time when I was in trouble, for deep down all was not as bright and breezy as I pretended it to be. I entitled it rather grandly: 'But in a Fiction'. But when I read it again the other day I was surprised how simply and truthfully it tells of some of the problems I faced at RADA and afterwards – it's so easy for drama students to become muddled with all the different theories and criticisms they are expected to absorb – so I include a few extracts from it here.

But in a Fiction

Is it not monstrous that this player here,
But in a fiction, in a dream of passion,
Could force his soul so to his own conceit
That from her working all his visage wann'd;
Tears in his eyes, distraction in's aspect,
A broken voice, and his whole function suiting
With forms to his conceit?

Hamlet

. . . unconscious creativeness through conscious technique.

Stanislavsky

Only connect.

E. M. Forster

Where's your continuity, dear?

Fabia Drake

12 July 1947

In my first term at RADA I was given the part of Leontes in *The Winter's Tale*; I was also the old shepherd, for which part I twisted my mouth, blinked my eyes, bent my back, croaked my voice – and convinced myself that I was fully in character! But in the same term I was given the part of Collins, the butler, in Shaw's *Getting*

Married. Here I could not be lost in emotion, as I was in Leontes, nor give a caricature, and the result was a stiff and dreadfully dull performance. For I had not learnt to point lines, to create a real character, to speak without emotion.

When I was staying at Ruth Winsten's at Ayot St Lawrence towards the end of term, we saw Bernard Shaw in his garden while were were out for a walk on the Sunday morning. He waved, and came to talk to us. It was sunny but very cold, and he was well wrapped up in plus-fours and a thick brown coat, and he had a large hat which he raised to us flamboyantly as he joined us in the lane. He was a friend of the Winstens so he walked with us for a while, and asked us which parts we had been given at RADA. Ruth told him hers, and when I told him mine he said, 'Ah yes. Collins is a much better part than Leontes. And of course *Getting Married* is a much better play than *The Winter's Tale!*'

We laughed. You could see our breaths.

'I'll tell you something about the part of Collins,' he said. 'I saw a performance of *Getting Married* years ago at the RADA and Collins was played by a fine young actor. But when I was talking to the students afterwards I had to tell him that he destroyed the balance of the play. "You're too good for the part," I said to him, "you stand out too much; you're not a member of a team." That young actor was Charles Laughton.'

We chatted some more about this and that and he inquired after Ruth's family. Mrs Winsten had done a statue of St Joan, which was in Shaw's garden. 'It's best to see it in the evening,' he said. 'She's got one hand raised, shielding her eyes from the sun. We've put her facing towards the west, so that on a sunny evening she really needs to have that hand to her eyes. Come into the garden and see it this evening if the sun's still out.' And with that he left us, raising his hat again. 'Good luck to all actors!' he said, and went off home.

*

In my second term we had Technique classes with Hugh Miller, who influenced my approach to acting very deeply. For him acting is not 'being', but 'seeming to be'. We were introduced to the art of acting for effect, learning such things as the rule 'look, move, speak', 'the aftersurge of emotion', 'moving on an arc', 'talking off a person'.

Here, perhaps, I made my biggest mistake. Even Hugh Miller put 'character', 'mood', and 'stage necessity' in that order. But from then on I have been tending to put 'stage necessity' first. From then on I have rarely 'felt' a performance – I have been so conscious of what every part of me has been doing, and of remembering all the little bits of business I had worked out during rehearsals.

I was often criticised for not being able to characterise fully – I was always too much myself. I was distressed by this criticism at the time, because I did not know what to do to remedy it, for I knew at last that 'character' was not distortion. My first part this term was Mr Crawley in *Scandal at Barchester*, and I had come up against the problem which still faces me as blankly as ever: what is the difference between Peter Barkworth mad and Mr Crawley mad, between Peter Barkworth angry and Mr Crawley angry? Or rather, how am I to express these differences? I still don't know. Strowan said my acting was a series of concepts: not a character at all, but me being angry, me being enthusiastic, me being in love with somebody.

I saw the truth of this at the time. But after having been produced by Ronald Kerr as Macbeth, I am not sure what is to be done. For Kerr's whole system of acting is based on one's own personality. For each character one tackles one asks the question not 'What is he?' but 'What am I?' One underlines certain aspects of one's own personality, never borrowing from outside, never striving for effect. One must never 'act'. One must 'be'. But surely one's own personality is not enough for the thousands of

characters one may have to portray? Surely one must ob-
serve others, and be able to 'tack on' business seen in other
people?

Maybe I've started all wrong. Maybe I've tried to be too like
Alec Guinness straight away. Now I hardly know the difference
between a technicality and a feeling, or whether an action is in
character or just for effect. I don't know where my acting is or
where it is going.

And we give our theatre performances of *Macbeth* the day after
tomorrow. Even today Ronnie Kerr said I was striving after effect
and he didn't believe in me at all. He said I had lost what I
previously had – though what that was I'm not at all sure.

Perhaps I have been 'playing' too much with too little thought
behind it, and about a week ago was getting too pleased with
myself, wondering how long I dare hold such and such a pause – I
counted up to fifteen once before I answered Lennox with 'Fled to
England?' I enjoyed listening to my own voice and exaggerated
some of my vocal mannerisms ('There the grown serpent *lll*lies'),
and I enjoyed 'acting nervous' with my eyes, especially in the first
scene in Act III, where I was trying to be master of Banquo yet
afraid of him. But today it all seemed hollow and empty and
nothing to do with Macbeth. It is too foreign a part for me. I am
tired of trying in vain to portray maturity and age, and am now
giving up in despair. I have no roughness necessary for Macbeth,
and am told I appear ridiculous.

31 July 1947

Macbeth was not a success; and I remember standing on the
platform at Goodge Street station, waiting for a tube to take me
home. It was the rush hour and there were lots of people around. I
was very disconsolate. But then I suddenly thought: 'No one on
this platform saw my awful performance this afternoon. It's not as
if we're doing things in public. What happens at RADA is in

private and only a handful of people saw it. And all these people, every single one of them, didn't. Thank God.'

And the train came and I was whisked away from Goodge Street towards Camden Town; and the further we went the happier I became.

In spite of that fiasco Ronnie Kerr asked me to play Young Woodley at his theatre, the Intimate, Palmers Green, to be directed by David Garth. I was told that I was suitable for the part, which did much to dispel my anxieties. It would be wonderful to play in a professional theatre again, and as it was to run for a week there would be plenty of time for experiment. Or so I thought.

Weekly rep allows but a little time for rehearsing and development. At the first rehearsal we just plotted the moves. Acting was not required. For the second day we had to know the lines of Act I, and we were expected to act so that David Garth could say something to us.

Well, he began by demonstrating nearly all my lines to me. I felt humiliated. Sometimes I felt stupid and ridiculous because I hadn't thought of quite an obvious way of saying a line or doing a gesture or a move, so I got more and more depressed. Not a good word was said, and I became defiant and adopted a don't-care attitude. I was rude to David. But this was merely a defence, covering up a real sense of inferiority. I was incapable of doing anything on the spur of the moment, and when everything is not worked out my movement becomes gawky and self-conscious, my voice mannerisms become ostentatious, my body becomes round-shouldered and my face sheepish and stupid.

So I went home and worked like the devil on Act II.

And on the Thursday morning he seemed more pleased and said a performance was in the making.

Act III, on the Friday, went all right until the frenzied 'Dare? . . . dare?' at the end of the first scene, where Woodley is screaming at Simmons in a great hysteria. I could not let myself go. I was shy of crying or of shouting, and miserably ashamed when David immediately produced a flood of tears and moved me profoundly with two words.

But on the first night I managed to remember all my lines and get some emotion across; and because my requirements of myself had grown gradually less during the week of rehearsals I was duly pleased with myself. Robert said considering it was weekly rep I wasn't too bad. 'The trouble with the others,' he said, 'is they're content with so little. It's as if they've said to themselves, "I know, I'll learn the lines and do the moves and wear the clothes and that's it!" And it's a bucketful of clichés. I mean: the man who's the schoolmaster: he shakes his head and his hands in a rather doddery way, speaks in a funny, clipped voice and calls it Mr Simmons. Even you, I mean, I can tell what you are going to do by the way you are standing . . . it's as though you've thought: "I know, hands in pockets mean I'm relaxed, hands behind back mean I'm defiant, a husky voice means I'm tense . . . I mean, they're all clichés.'

'That's David,' I said, disloyally, 'he told me to do them. And do you know, Robert, he wouldn't let me act with my back to the audience . . . he wouldn't let me turn away upstage when I was hurt by Laura. "No – all your reactions *must* be out front," he said. Somebody else there laughed when I protested.'

'Well, I suppose dogmatic methods are essential in this ghastly business of weekly rep,' said Robert, grandly.

'I suppose so,' I said.

'I can remember lots of your lines, though,' he said, 'and that's good.'

'Yes it is,' I said pleased.

'The only thing is I can see you are straining for effects instead of just being immersed in the part. It's too . . .' and he paused, 'too *acted*.'

'Yes, I see,' I said, crestfallen.

7 August 1947

I am at home for the holidays now and this afternoon went to Dorothea Alexander's for tea and told her of my difficulties.

'Oh, you're bound to feel wretched and awkward at times when you're learning so fast,' she said sympathetically. 'You're on show all the time, you see. Don't worry. It's the same for everyone. I bet you think they're all much more confident than you, but they won't be, inside. Don't worry. And don't worry too much about mannerisms. As long as your stock of them is continually increasing, so that too much repetition is avoided, and as long as they are good and expressive, mannerisms are necessary for a professional performance, and are the actor's own personal idiom.'

We also talked of approach. And she is right. I have not been thinking deeply enough about character. She suggests that next time I read the play more, and not hurry over lines and business (this, of course, is what Strowan has been saying for months – I've been a fool, I suppose). She said I should keep to the book as long as possible, find out everything about the character's background, past life, environment and relationships with the other characters. Only then should I start to think of the lines and of what I can convey by them. I must work more slowly, she said, and not expect instant results. I must be more sparing, and only use a gesture and a look when it really means something. She is a great believer in stillness on the stage.

She suggested that besides jotting down things I notice in people, I should listen carefully to and make notes of conversations I hear. I should include an hour every week as part of my timetable to go somewhere with the set purpose of watching and listening to people. 'A cathedral, or a park bench, or a shop,' she said.

She gave me a new voice exercise too, to improve my low notes. I had to intone, very slowly, 'Nine kneeling nuns know neither needle nor knitting', prolonging the 'n' sound at the beginning of each word until the tongue started to tingle, and then opening up at last to let the vowel sing out, and going lower and lower each time until I'd come to the bottom of my voice. 'Do it every day, and try going a semi-tone even lower from time to time,' she said. 'Your low notes are not good. They need strength.'

And she emphasized again the value of repose. 'In particular relax your hands,' she said. 'They're too fidgety.'

28 August 1947

It was both entertaining and instructive to see *A Sleeping Clergyman* at the Criterion, with Robert Donat playing Cameron, the part I did at RADA last term.

I was astounded by the depth of his imagination, how everything he did seemed to spring from thinking about the character. He made me remember the quotation at the beginning of Forster's *Howard's End*: 'Only connect.' How Robert Donat connected! Whenever he was thinking of his work as a scientist he pinned his thoughts down on to the microscope and scientific instruments in his room. He *used* them: they were his pegs. They became the encapsulation of the whole of his work.

2 December 1947

Alec Guinness, in *An Inspector Calls*, had one of the most revealing bits of business I have ever seen. He had to show the audience he was a drink addict without being drunk and without even having a drink. He walked past the sideboard, which had several bottles on it. He stopped, faltered, and touched one of the bottles. Then, when he saw someone was looking at him, he just pushed it away from him, very slightly. That was all. We saw him do it, and we knew what he was feeling: it was his character in a nutshell.

10 January 1948

Strowan was again a huge help with *Much Ado About Nothing*, when I was Benedick in the first half.

'Boy!' I had to say, at the beginning of the orchard scene, 'In my chamber window lies a book: bring it hither to me i' the orchard.'

'No,' said Strowan, as I enunciated the lines crisply and carefully, 'you know exactly where the book is. See it in your mind's eye and just *tell* the boy to go for it.'

Then I had to say: 'I do much wonder that one man, seeing how much another man is a fool when he dedicates his behaviours to love, will, after he hath laughed at such shallow follies in others, become the argument of his own scorn by falling in love . . .'

'That,' said Strowan, interrupting me, 'is a *general* opinion.'

'Mm, mm,' I said, agreeing, and went on, 'And such a man is Claudio.'

'And that,' said Strowan, 'is a *particular* one. You must see Claudio in your mind, know where he is. Is he where you've just come from?'

'Could be,' I said, vaguely, not really knowing.

'Well, just turn your head in that direction! Yes, that's good. It makes Claudio come to life.'

But a few days after we'd done our performance of *Much Ado*, I saw Fabia Drake at a bus-stop in Tottenham Court Road. She called me over. 'Peter Barkworth,' she said, 'I've seen you do three things this term and they've all been Peter Barkworth. Now where's your sense of character?'

I had had a most depressing day; I looked stupid and said, 'Yes – er – has it disappeared altogether, Miss Drake?'

'Well I doubt if it ever existed, Peter, but really you've got to do something, or you'll be very handicapped.'

'Oh . . .'

'And another thing,' she said, looking to see if her bus was coming. It wasn't, unfortunately. 'Your comedy technique requires tuition and experiment. You do not know when a line is good enough to leave, or when it requires extra business to get a laugh.'

'Yes, I see,' I said. I didn't at all. 'Thank you, Miss Drake.' I was getting cross and wanted to go.

'Don't be down-hearted, Peter. You're going to be a good actor. But you've got to work harder, you know. And RADA is the place to do that. You're going to join the Army when you've finished here, aren't you? Well, that'll be good for you. It'll broaden your attitudes and develop your personality. For now, just keep on working, and never stop experimenting.'

Her bus had come.

'Goodbye, Peter dear.'

'Goodbye, Miss Drake. Thank you.'

And I felt strangely elated, as though I knew everything would perhaps come right, after all, in the end.

26 February 1949

I wrote my last entry here, over a year ago now, on the train from Stockport to London. I was returning after the Christmas holidays for my fifth term at RADA, the term of the Public Show. Now that I am in the Army and feel so far away, that term seems to me like a world of dreams; at the time it was the hardest slog of hard-slog work I have ever done. For the first three weeks of it we did a production under Fabia Drake of an awkward comedy: *This Woman Business*, by Benn Levy.

Fabia taught us how to point lines, pausing to feel for an operative word, doing nonchalant actions, like scratching one's forehead or wiping cigarette ash from one's lap, to emphasize the nonchalance of a nonchalant line, and even how to do a double take. She said comedy acting requires utter relaxation and the perfect balance between projection and undercut. She could make us roar with laughter at her use of these technical aids, often without any words. She would just hum the build and the undercut and have us in stitches:

De dar de dar DE DAR DE DAR –
<small>de dar de dar de dar</small>

I was often severely chastised by her, though; particularly on account of my diction. I had always rather prided myself on my diction but it was certainly not up to the technical efficiency needed for playing light comedy. One day she made me feel utterly miserable by shouting at me the whole morning that she couldn't hear what I was saying. I went home that evening (I still lived at Regent's Park Road then) and worked on my voice and diction for several hours. Yesterday I met a young chap who is going to be a pianist, and he practises seven hours a day. An actor has an equal amount of technical skill to acquire and to maintain: the voice must be perfect, diction flawless, the body must be healthy and in supple trim and the mind must be awake and alert. It is horribly easy to allow some of these things to slip.

I shall always be grateful to Fabia. She taught me more than anyone else I have known. She was brutally frank in her criticism and spared no feelings. I have seen her make people cry. But she is a brilliant producer for students and I'm sorry she is not still teaching at RADA.

It was about this time that I was called into Miss Brown's office. 'Peter dear,' she said, 'come and sit down. I want to talk to you.' She sounded awfully solemn and horsey and I wondered what I had done.

She was sitting at her desk. She put her pen down and turned to face me. 'I saw *This Woman Business* when you did it in the Little Theatre the other day. And I thought you were very good. As good as you've been here. Now, I'm glad about that, because I think comedy is what you should concentrate on. I think you're going to have to be a comic actor, you see, because' – and she paused – 'you've got a funny face. It's a nice face, but it's not conventionally good-looking. It's funny.'

'Thank you for telling me, Miss Brown,' I said, not knowing what to think.

'I hope you don't mind; I just felt I wanted to. Now run along dear, and I hope you get the part you want in the Public Show. The auditions are next week you know.'

The Public Show! It was not the end of our course but it was certainly the climax. How we buzzed and babbled about it in the classrooms and corridors! *Everybody* would be there: agents (most important), managements, directors, producers, friends and families and famous people. It was our shop window: we would be on display to the profession and written about in the newspapers the following day. This year, 1948, it was to be held in the afternoon at the St James's Theatre. The judges would be Sybil Thorndike, Sophie Stewart, Leslie Banks, Basil Dean and Alan Dent.

I was tried for two parts: Ninian in *The First Mrs Fraser*, and the Captain in a short play written specially for the Public Show by Hugh Miller called *Dark Sentence*. I wanted Ninian: it was a light comedy part, and my own age. The part of the Captain did not interest me much and I worked very hard indeed at Ninian. At the trials I was selected for it and was thus given a great chance, for commercially I couldn't have asked for anything better.

The play, or rather the first act of it, which was all we did, was produced by Ursula Jeans. Following Fabia's tuition in light comedy I was able to get some of the points across, but was greatly helped in a lot of sticky things by Miss Jeans. I remember her insistence on naturalism. 'No,' she would say, after having given one of us a move, 'that *looks* like a move . . . now what can we do to make it look absolutely spontaneous?' And we would try different timing, or different placing, or try to cover up the move with some other business. She was a great one, too, for motivation. At one point I had to cross the stage for a cigarette. Before I crossed I ought to convey to the audience, she said, (a) that I wanted a cigarette, (b) that I hadn't got one on me and (c) that I knew there were some in the box on the mantelpiece.

Ursula Jeans was full of wonderful tips. For instance she said that anything which annoys the audience or raises their curiosity in a wrong place is to be avoided; she maintained that if an actor puts his foot on a chair half the audience will be worrying about whether he has dirtied it or not.

She helped me to get lightness of touch, and was the first person to bring out any sparkle in me. 'You should be like champagne, Peter,' she said, 'lively, sparkly, brilliant.' She told me I fidget with my elbows when my hands are in my pockets. She showed me the value of a minute pause before an important line (particularly a cutting one).

Anyway the result of it all was that I was awarded a Judges' Special Medal at the Public Show (that was a day!). That meant I'd come fourth. Brewster Mason was first with the Gold Medal, Leora Dana second with the Silver and Peter Sallis third with the Bronze. I was offered a job the next day: to play the lead in *The Guinea Pig* at Folkestone for the Arthur Brough Players. I had to ask permission of course, but as it was now the Easter holidays it was granted readily.

So the following Sunday I packed my bags and caught the train from Charing Cross. It was a journey I was to get to know very well, with the two noisy tunnels on either side of Sevenoaks, and the long, straight bit between Tonbridge and Ashford, where the train charges recklessly through orchards and hopfields. I had never seen the Weald of Kent before, although I'd read about it in Siegfried Sassoon's books, and it seemed to me the most beautiful place in the world. And Folkestone was certainly the most beautiful seaside town, with the Leas Pavilion theatre tucked in

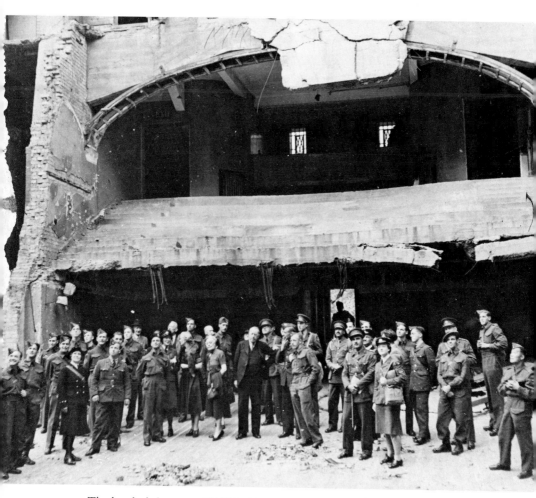

The bombed theatre at RADA. Sir Kenneth Barnes in the centre, Dame Irene Vanbrugh by his side. When the theatre was rebuilt it was named after her.

A RADA *production of* Julius Caesar.
*Robert Shaw is top left, with me below
him, imploring Caesar, with other forgotten
faces.*

*Home for the Christmas holidays,
with Hazel.*

The prize-winners after the Public Show in 1948. Standing, left to right, are Maidé Nolte, David Ashman, Pam Galloway, Theodore Bikel, Cherry Morris, me, Hilda Braid, John Jones and James Kier. Sitting are Edna Fryer, Brewster Mason, Peter Sallis and Alan Nunn. Where had Leora Dana disappeared to?

(Central Press)

With Peter Walter in
The Guinea Pig at Folkestone.

The whole company in The Guinea Pig, *with Arthur Brough and*
Elizabeth Addyman (Mrs Brough) on the left.

between hotels at the top of the cliffs. I found some splendid digs, called Wulfruna House, where they didn't mind if I practised out loud.

One of the luckiest things of all was that the company at Folkestone was really good: hard-working, dedicated and talkative. Well, I have always liked talking about acting, but I don't think I've ever got so much from conversations as I did there: from Mary Russell, the solid character actress, from Mr Brough himself, with his impeccable comedy timing and – his greatest feat – his marvellous way of being preoccupied with his own thoughts, and from Peter Walter, who had such a splendid grasp of how to work in a weekly rep. He was the leading man, and on matinée days I would sometimes go in early to talk to him and pick his brains.

'Yes,' he told me, 'I use rehearsals to work out what I am going to do. I work on the lines and their meaning of course; and I work out what my movements will be, especially where I will *look* – at the other characters, or at no one in particular – and what my hands are doing.'

'Yes. I know. I see you do,' I said. He was a clean and clear actor with a fine sense of comedy. He was, I thought, immaculate. Starry, even.

'But in performance,' he said emphatically, 'I try to forget about everything except the *thoughts* of the character. I forget about technique, moves, interpretation, even the words as just *words*. The basis of all playing must be relaxation. When you know what you are doing you can relax and be confident; and only when your whole concentration is on the thoughts of the character can real personality zoom over the footlights and capture the house.'

The Guinea Pig was so successful that I was asked to stay on at Folkestone for four more plays during the remainder of the RADA holidays.

In *The Shop at Sly Corner* I had a lot of scenes with Mr Brough, so of course he saw every performance of mine. I thought I was quite good in the part of Archie the blackmailer but I learned afterwards that he didn't. I thought I was good because I'd invented a lot of business but Brough said I was too theatrical and mechanical. 'I could see,' he said, 'that you had planned to put your elbow on the table on that word and your chin on your fist on that word. It wasn't that you had planned it that was wrong, for a lot of things have to be planned, but that it *looked* as if you had planned it. You're far too exact. Far too *careful*.'

I came a cropper on the first night of *Love in Idleness*. It was a vast part and I just didn't seem to have time to do it, what with having to do *The Shop at Sly Corner* every night and on Wednesday, Friday and Saturday afternoons. I remember being awful at rehearsals, struggling over lines and not knowing what to do. I stayed in the whole of Sunday to be sure I knew it, and the dress rehearsal on the Monday morning went smoothly enough. But alas, at the first performance in the evening I could hardly remember a line of the first act. I was tired out and my brain wouldn't function. Peter Walter and Elizabeth Addyman had to prompt me, or put my lines in the form of questions like 'Were you going to tell us that . . . ?' or 'Haven't you got anything to say about . . . ?' which they were adept at doing. In fact my marvelling at their cleverness made me dry even more. It was the stuff of which nightmares are made.

And when I woke up on Tuesday morning I still didn't know it and had to learn it all over again. But the second night was better than the first and by the end of the week I was enjoying myself. Then we did another week of *The Guinea Pig*, by public demand, and it was loudly acclaimed all over again. There were cheers, even.

After all this my last term at RADA was a sad anticlimax. I immersed myself in exams for the London University Diploma in Dramatic Art. Only Robert and I passed. I had three Distinctions: in Acting, Diction and French. But it was all very dull.

The only bright spot was when we went to Alexandra Palace to do a short play for television. It was called *Rahab*, by Gordon Daviot. I had a very tiny part as a guard on the walls of Jericho. Barbara Jefford was Rahab, a tart whom I captured. I was very nervous and can't remember at all how I played it, but I liked being in a television studio and it was nice not having to speak up. In fact Barbara and I did most of it in a whisper. And when later we came to do the same play again, but this time on a cart in Russell Square, to an audience who just stood around, we collapsed with laughter because of having to shout it. The contrast was too much and it all seemed false and dreadful. I noticed my knees were dirty, too, and that didn't help. Sir Kenneth wasn't at all pleased and ticked us off afterwards.

As soon as I had left RADA I was asked to return to Folkestone where, it was generally agreed, I improved out of all recognition. Suddenly I was able to act with much greater freedom. I did what I planned to do still, but somehow at each performance new things happened and I had the confidence to let them and to stray along unknown paths. It was a beautiful feeling. I was relaxing and trying to think the thoughts of the character, leaving other considerations at the back of my mind. Even First Night nerves had by now practically disappeared.

But in October I had to leave to do my year and a half of National Service.

Goodbyes were sad. Brough said again how I had improved since I first joined him for *The Guinea Pig* because I was less mechanical. He said he would keep a place for me in the company for when I came out of the Army. This was a godsend and took a lot of the pain out of leaving. I had a job to come back to! How lucky! How fortunate!

'Yes,' said Mr Brough, pleased that I was so pleased, 'all you have to do is let me know when you're going to be demobbed, and a job will be waiting for you. Goodbye Peter. Good luck! Try not to hate the Army too much. Though you'll be glad, I know, and so will we, when it's over.'

After a few months' absence I went back-stage in a theatre last night. How I miss the urgency and the thrill, the joys of making-up and stepping out on to the stage and speaking so that 'all shall hear'. How I miss the intensity of living in the theatre, of creating a character from nothing but the printed page, of living a life 'but in a fiction'.

Dismissed

I rather enjoyed the Army, especially after I was commissioned. That made life a lot easier: I could have a room to myself, carry a cane, slacken my salute, and drape. 'The trouble with you, Barkworth,' my C.O. at Officer Cadet School had said, 'is that you drape. You lean against things instead of standing upright. Never mind, you've done well. You knew nothing at all when you came here, and now you know quite a lot. I can't give you an A but I'm going to give you a B plus. Congratulations!' And he shook my hand.

And thanks to him I got the posting I wanted: to a Heavy Ack-Ack practice camp at Weybourne on the north coast of Norfolk. Soon after I arrived I was given three pleasant jobs which had nothing to do with all the expensive training I had received at Cadet School. I was to be a Battery Commander, in charge of about sixty batmen, cooks, clerks, drivers and orderlies; Entertainments Officer for the whole camp, in which capacity I had to organize concerts, film-shows and dances in a vast hangar with a corrugated iron roof and a bare stage at the far end; and secretary of the Officers' Mess, which meant running what was really a small hotel, but one which, thank heavens, didn't have to make money. All very cushy, I thought.

There were some awful moments, though. Like when a very

important major-general came to take the salute at a big parade and had to be entertained afterwards to luncheon in our Mess. I had gone to a great deal of trouble to make sure the meal would be perfect; but in order to make life not too difficult for the chef I had agreed to his suggestion that the first course should be tomato soup. Unhappily he had not noticed that the labels on the large tins which he had bought said that it was concentrated, and needed to be diluted '6 parts milk or water to 1 part soup'.

The officers sat talking gently amongst themselves while the steaming stuff was served. I thought it looked a bit dark, but decided to ignore it. The major-general lifted his spoon and fifty or more obedient officers watched, and followed suit. And together they tasted, heaved and spewed. Some of the junior officers laughed. I signalled to the sergeant-in-charge to have the plates removed, and went into the kitchen to lose my temper and hide. When I emerged the junior officers smirked and looked away, but Colonel Wall, our C.O., was not amused. 'The officer always has to take the blame,' he said to me, seriously, afterwards.

Soon after that I was organizing a regimental dance and had hired, at considerable expense, four coaches to bring girls in from nearby towns and villages. But the coaches came back empty because somebody had got the date wrong. An appalling evening ensued. The band went on playing because they felt they had to, and a few men decided to dance together; but they soon gave up, red-faced on account of the jeers of their less adventurous mates. Soon the only couple left on the floor in that huge barn of a building was the luckless Colonel Wall and his wife.

When it was over, and the band was paid, I repaired to the Mess and got drunk.

Mrs Wall liked to organize the social life of the young officers, and formed the M.M. (Mainly Military) Club, which met once a month in a small hall in Sheringham. All the junior officers were expected to attend, and desirable young ladies from Holt,

Sheringham and Cromer were invited as guests, to eat sandwiches and drink sherry. The dreariness of these evenings was beyond belief and we nearly cried with the stifling boredom of it all. Soon we would go to any lengths to excuse ourselves from attending, inventing important duties to be done at the camp, or illness, or, in one desperate case, bereavement. Eventually the club was disbanded, and Mrs Wall said she thought we were 'an unsociable lot of young officers, and very disappointing'.

On the whole, though, the days and nights at Weybourne passed pleasantly enough. I was fully occupied and very healthy. In my spare time I went for long walks by the sea, and dreamed of being back at Folkestone. I realized I had very little talent for organizing meals or dances or concerts, and consequently didn't do them very well. But I noticed I was readily forgiven for my errors and forgetfulness on the grounds that I was an actor, and therefore something of an odd-ball, a figure of fun. They laughed at me, but the laughter was tinged with admiration: I had chosen to be an actor, and although I had hardly started, I was already at one remove from them in their eyes, and would, with luck, eventually inhabit a world far more romantic than they would ever know. They liked to hear about RADA and Folkestone and stories of the stars, and I knew that any pleasure I derived from being in the Army was because I wasn't really a soldier at all: I was an actor playing the part of one.

My best audience for all this showing off was Gerald Harper. He hadn't started at all yet, but his demob was coming up before mine and I coached him a bit for his auditions at RADA. It was my first experience of teaching; I was proud of him and of myself when he got in.

Not everybody likes actors. A distinguished author once said to me that he found actors, on the whole, 'boring, conceited and empty-headed'. But fortunately most people do seem to like us, and we exude a fascination for them which is often ill deserved.

But, I have to admit, I love it. I like not being anonymous. I am proud of the profession I am in and have no wish to keep it a secret. Oh there are times when it can be irritating, when people are too familiar and inquisitive, or demand a long conversation and ask to take a photograph at the end of it; and there can be too much touching and pawing and shaking of hands, and sometimes a considerable amount of rudeness, especially from youthful gangs, who giggle if they are girls and jeer if they are boys. But these annoyances are a small price to pay for the admiring glances and friendly words which keep us sustained and happy. And of course it is very pleasant to be looked after well in shops and restaurants and hotels, and when travelling about in trains and aeroplanes. For all the changes of style in plays, films and television programmes, actors and actresses are still just as glamorous and just as talked and written about as ever they were, and long may it continue!

I was early for the train which would take me back to Folkestone from Charing Cross. I had been out of the Army for a fortnight and my hair was growing longer again. I was glad to be out: the last few weeks had dragged painfully. I walked the length of the platform to where it emerges from under the huge station roof and projects out towards the river until you can stand right over the noisy traffic rattling its way along the Embankment. It was a perfect April evening. The busy river looked as it does in Canaletto's pictures, and St Paul's was turning orange in the setting sun. I was free again. And I was in London. One day I shall act here, I thought, looking round. The certainty and fervour with which I thought it astonished me.

And when I was sitting in the train, heaving once more across the darkening Weald of Kent, I stared out of the window feeling strangely powerful, knowing that my return to Folkestone was only the beginning, only part of a pattern which would evolve slowly, like a spiral twisting gently outwards.

Ashford, Sandling-for-Hythe, Westernhanger. Impatient now: would we never get there? I took my cases down from the rack and sat with them by my side. At long last we drew into Folkestone Central. The air was sharper than in London; and overhead the herring-gulls squawked at each other, and a full moon shone out of a pitch-black sky. I struggled with my cases to my new digs in Ingles Road, and hurriedly unpacked my things and said hello, and yes, I would like to have supper, but could it be in about half an hour, because I just wanted to walk as far as the Leas? Fine, they said, so I went out, but I didn't walk, I ran, right to the cliff top, and looked out to sea.

A shaft of silver moonlight sparkled away from me to the horizon. France was just over there, ships moved imperceptibly across the black, deep water, and the flashing light from the wall of Dover harbour was as insistent as ever. The pine trees on the cliff face beneath me smelt of incense as they always had done. It was all so familiar it was as though I had never been away. I stood there for some time, quite still, taking it all in. Then I turned round and looked at the little theatre behind me, snug between the hotels. The evening's performance was still going on: the lights outside looked inviting, but I didn't go in, or wait for the performance to be over so that I could meet all the actors. I didn't want to speak to anyone. I walked slowly back to Ingles Road and ate my supper and went to bed.

I was back.

Hellos the following morning were loud and jolly, and everybody seemed pleased to see me. There were quite a lot of faces I knew, but there were some new ones too, so introductions were quickly made, and at ten o'clock, on the dot, we started to rehearse. The play was *Master of Arts* and I can now remember nothing about it whatsoever. I kept no diary at Folkestone, and have no records: no press-cuttings, no programmes, no copies of any of the plays. Maybe I had them once and threw them away after I had left, in an effort to forget the dreadful thing that was to happen.

My memory of that summer of 1950 has become very blurred: a series of unconnected images, vague and out of sequence, but with a few clear moments coming and going, like the picture on a faulty television set. Sun on the Leas (that mile of greensward at the top of the cliffs), the zig-zag path, the picturesque road leading down to the harbour, the view of Shakespeare Cliff on the far side of the Warren; and the little Edwardian theatre with its musty pocket-handkerchief stage; at rehearsals, when we weren't in a scene, we would sit on the stairs at the back of the auditorium and watch, and Mr Brough, who directed all the plays, would stand in the centre aisle, smoking his pipe and making a note or two.

Arthur Brough, who years later was to be so funny and touching in the BBC comedy series *Are You Being Served?*, was a small, slightly stout man with an unlined boyish face. He was homely and spoke slowly, with a country burr. He was hardly ever without a pipe in his hand and liked to smoke it on the stage whenever he could. He was called Peter by his friends, which I always thought was confusing. Mrs Brough, whose stage name was Elizabeth Addyman but who was called Bess by her friends, was elegant, flute-voiced and nervous.

In my memory the evening performances were always full, but no one ever came back-stage afterwards, or waited at the stage door. The cold night air outside was a shock after the heat of that cramped little theatre, and after the show we would stand on the deserted Leas to cool off and gossip. Then we would say goodnight and go our separate ways. I don't remember ever going out for a meal, or even a drink, after the show.

On three afternoons a week, at 3.45, tea matinées were given. Every alternate row of seats was taken out and tables were put in their place. Afternoon tea was ordered, served, consumed, cleared away and paid for during the performances, and we giggled shamelessly, especially during tense parts. It was more than we could bear to hear a Folkestone matron hissing, 'Waitress . . . waitress . . . more hot water please,' or the chink, chink of money on a plate as the waitress counted out the change in the dark, ever so slowly: 'That's one . . . two . . . three . . . and sixpence,' and the reply: 'Thanks very much and that's for you.'

An endurance test for us, the tea matinées were; nevertheless, they were popular and well attended. Mr and Mrs Brough were the king and queen of Folkestone and their little theatre gleamed. 'Oh they're so lovely, the Broughs,' people would say when they recognized me on the Leas and stopped for a chat, 'and Mrs Brough is *charming* isn't she?'

It was fun being recognized. It was my first taste of it. The Leas were at their fullest when people came out of church on Sunday mornings, and I used to make a point of stopping work on the next play and going out for a walk at about noon to catch the rush, hoping secretly I would be recognized a lot. In the afternoon, if the weather was fair, I would compensate by going for a long solitary walk on the downs behind the town, and test myself to see if I could mutter all my lines for the following play, in sequence, without the help of the other people's cues. If I could, it meant I really knew it.

The plays flitted by: *Quiet Weekend, Night Was Our Friend, Off the Record*; and the Arthur Brough Players were *en fête*, for this was the year of their twenty-first anniversary, which was to be celebrated with a special production of *The School for Scandal* in October.

But in June I had received a letter from Peter Sallis.

When one lives the day-to-day, often hand-to-mouth, existence of a freelance actor, everything can be changed, in an instant, by a telephone call or a letter. The suddenness can be quite disturbing. 'Are you free on Friday to fly to Spain for three months' filming?' was one such call I received; 'Will you come to Perth to do *Present Laughter* for a season?' was in a recent letter from Australia. A moment ago one had no work: suddenly there's an offer. One was free: now one is not.

Peter Sallis told me in his letter that the juvenile actor at the Sheffield Playhouse was leaving, so there was a vacancy. It was a fully fortnightly rep (Folkestone was fortnightly only in midsummer – in spring and autumn it was weekly) with a good standard. Was I interested? If so, he would recommend me to the director, Geoffrey Ost. I wrote back to say thank you, but Arthur Brough had kept this job open for me for the year and a half I had been in the Army and I could hardly turn round now, after only three months, and say sorry, I'm off.

That's that, I thought, relieved, as I posted my reply.

But about a month later, while we were rehearsing for *Black Chiffon*, I was talking to Kate Sawtell, who was Brough's secretary, in the courtyard of the theatre just outside his office, and I told her about Peter Sallis's letter and what I had done about it.

'Oh Peter,' she said quietly, looking round to see we were not being overheard, 'I know I shouldn't say this and I'm being disloyal, but you're a fool. It's wonderful there. I came here from there. Isn't that strange? But it's wonderful,' she repeated, and fell silent. She was small, and had a rosy face and wispy hair.

'Better than here?' I asked.

'In a different class altogether,' she said, and then, hurriedly, 'I mean here's good, don't get me wrong, but Sheffield is one of the major reps in the country. After Birmingham and Liverpool probably the most important. Oh dear. It would have done you so much good . . .'

'But I couldn't have left here after such a short time.'

'In this world you have to look after yourself. Offers like this don't grow on trees.'

'Oh no, it's not an offer. It's just a suggestion.'

'Well, if it's just a suggestion there would be no harm in writing to Peter Sallis to see if the job's still going, would there?'

'It's probably gone,' I said, more hopefully than sadly.

'No harm in asking,' Kate whispered conspiratorially, and went back into the office.

Within an hour my letter was posted, and I walked the length of the Leas to Sandgate and back.

Peter replied: the job was still free. He had talked to Geoffrey Ost, who would like to meet me at the offices of The Spotlight in about a fortnight. 'You could fix a time for the interview by telephoning Geoffrey here.'

So I did. There was nothing I could do now, I decided, except go along with it. Let events decide. Perhaps Geoffrey Ost might not like me, might prefer somebody else. I told Kate what I had done. She was pleased, and couldn't understand why I was so unenthusiastic. The next day, Brough called me into his office. Kate was there, working at her desk. 'Peter,' said Brough genially, his hand on my shoulder, 'I've got a confession to make: there's no part for you in the play after *Black Chiffon*; and in Bess's play, which follows that, there's only a very small part indeed. I'm sorry about this. So look. Bess agrees there's no need for you to come to the first week of rehearsals for her play, so would you like a week's holiday? You've got some enormous parts coming up in *The School for Scandal* and other plays, so you could recharge your batteries.'

I thought for a moment. The week's holiday coincided with my interview with Geoffrey Ost, which was to be on the Monday. Then I could go home and talk it over with my parents. Suddenly I needed them very badly.

'That's nice of you,' I said. 'Yes. Thank you.'

Kate and I exchanged no looks. I felt terribly furtive, and said nothing about my plans.

The interview in London was pleasant, and Geoffrey Ost said he'd let me know when he'd seen everyone he wanted to see. I went home to Bramhall, and he telephoned me on the Thursday to say the job was mine if I wanted it. I said yes I did, and he told me when I should start. It was settled in two minutes.

There was ample time for me to give in the twenty-eight days' notice which my contract stipulated. Nevertheless I decided to cut my holiday short and return to Folkestone the following day. I telephoned Mr Brough to ask if he would see me after the show on Friday night. 'Yes,' he said, surprised, come and see me at home.'

It was half past ten when I rang his bell.

'Come in,' he said. And after we had sat: 'What do you want to tell me?'

I told him what had happened.

'So,' I said, 'and I hate doing this, I've come to say, can I give in my twenty-eight days' notice? Can I leave after *The School for Scandal?*'

He had listened in silence, and the silence continued when I had stopped. He got up, relit his pipe, and poured himself a drink without offering me one. Oh Christ, I thought.

'No,' he said at last, pacing about. 'No, I will not accept your notice. I engaged you for the season and you know it. We had a verbal agreement that you were to be here for the whole season, whatever the contract says. No. You may not go.'

'Well,' I said lamely, 'I've said I will.'

'Then you'll have to unsay it,' he said.

'I don't see how I can,' I said.

'How much is he paying you?'

'Eight pounds.'

'Eight pounds?' he exploded. 'But that's exactly what you get here. Why do you want to go?'

I couldn't say because I've heard it's better, so I kept quiet.

'I don't understand you,' he went on, getting loud. 'Haven't you been happy here?'

'Very.'

'Well then?'

'Well, it's apparently got a very high standard.'

'Not as high as it is here, I can promise you that.'

Again I was silent. I didn't know what to say.

But he did. He was really warming up: 'Never in my twenty-one years' experience in rep has anyone behaved so badly to me as you are doing now.' He was to say this often. 'And when I think that I kept this job open for you all the time you were in the Army, and you turn round and slap me in the face like you've just done, I have to tell you I have never been more angry with anyone in my life. I gave you a holiday, and you used it to get yourself another job.'

'Well, no, it wasn't quite like that.'

'I refuse to accept your notice. Get out of that if you can. That's all. Good night.'

I heard nothing from him during the weekend. On Monday I was due to rehearse in Mrs Brough's play, which was called *Fortunes in a Teacup*.

At eight o'clock on Monday morning the telephone rang at my digs. 'It's for you, Peter,' said my landlady.

'I require to see you before rehearsal in my office. Be there at a quarter to ten,' and he put the telephone down without waiting for a reply.

I was there on the dot. Kate was looking very drawn. 'Never in my twenty-one years here . . .' he started, as though there had been no gap in our conversation. 'It's the disloyalty of it all that has astounded me. Why didn't you tell me what you were planning to do? How dare you come back here and present me with a *fait accompli*!'

'If I had told you,' I said, 'you would have dissuaded me from going.'

'Yes, I probably would,' he admitted.

'That's why I didn't,' I said truthfully.

'What I can't understand is why you want to go from here.'

'It's not that I want to go from here. I'm grateful for everything you've done. But I want to go there.'

'Well then,' he said, 'I can't stop you.' It was nearly ten o'clock. 'But just let me say one thing finally: even if you were to pay me, I would never ever have you back here.'

He was, as usual, the director of the play. We had somehow to get through the rehearsal, so I was glad I was in only one scene of it. He told me what the moves were. When we went through the scene a couple of times afterwards, he stood in his usual place in the centre aisle, but he turned his back on the stage.

That evening there was another telephone call. He told me to present myself at his office the following morning at 9.30.

'First of all,' he said when I got there, his voice hoarse with tiredness, 'I have to tell you I cannot stand the sight of you around the place, and I do not want you to be in my wife's play. Nor, as it happens, does she.'

'Oh,' I said, stunned.

'I want you to go. Now. Contractually I am supposed to pay you for four more weeks. But I don't want to. I don't want to give you another penny. But you have to agree to that.'

'All right,' I said, 'I don't want any more money from you.'

'I don't want to see you again. I want you to leave Folkestone today.'

'I can't,' I said.

'Why?'

'Well. There are people to say goodbye to. And I've promised to take my landlady to the concert at the Leas Cliff Hall on Sunday. I won't leave before then.'

He seemed to ignore this. 'Another thing. I haven't been at all pleased with your work.' This was a nasty stab in the back, and I knew it. He had never hinted at anything like this before. 'You are not nearly as good now as you were when you first came here.'

Even Kate looked shocked at his malevolence. She turned back to a letter she had been typing. Brough took his cue from her. 'Kate has been typing a letter I've dictated, and I'm going to send copies of it to Equity, to RADA, and to Geoffrey Ost at Sheffield, complaining of your behaviour and giving my frank opinion of you. Kate. Read it to him.'

Kate read his long, vituperative letter. When she had finished, he said, 'Have you anything to say?'

'Well . . . no,' I said eventually.

'That's all,' he said, quietly, and opened the door for me. As I walked out of his office, he banged the door savagely in my back, which sent me sprawling on the terrace outside.

I saw him once more while I remained at Folkestone. He and his wife were also at the concert at the Leas Cliff Hall, and by an unhappy coincidence their seats were in the same row as mine. They were standing in the centre aisle as my landlady and I arrived. They had to move to let us pass. They turned their backs as they did so.

The following morning I left Folkestone.

Discovered

Kate was right: The Playhouse, Sheffield, was in a different league; but I was never to feel as attached to it as I had been to the little Leas Pavilion at the top of the cliffs. I was in a city now, instead of a soft seaside town. I had to travel to work by bus or by tram, and the office blocks got higher and the shop windows larger as we climbed the slow hill to the city centre.

My heart was thumping, my first morning, as I got off at the Grand Hotel, bought *The Times* and the *Sheffield Telegraph* from a kiosk on the corner, and put them in my briefcase to read later. A road or two to cross at the traffic lights, down the little hill of Townhead Street, and then into the theatre through the box-office, passing two ten-by-eight photographs of myself in a single large frame. I always gave it a glance as I went in, and read my name.

The interior of the theatre was dignified, and hushed like a library. The actors had their heads buried in their scripts as they sat in the darkness of the wings, or round the edge of the stage. They looked up and said, 'Good morning', and I shook hands with them all and sat with Peter Sallis. It wasn't quite ten o'clock yet, so everybody went on whispering or reading.

'How are you?' said Peter.

'Well,' I said.

'Welcome,' he said.

'Thank you,' I said.

Geoffrey Ost got up and said, 'Let's start now please,' and stood with his back to the curtain, which was down. (It had been a sideways one at Folkestone, and wafted about in the draughts there; but here it was an up-and-down one and made of much stronger stuff, so it didn't waft at all.) He gave the actors in the opening scenes their moves, very quietly, from notes he had written in the margin of his script.

What impressed me was that they all seemed to know what to do without talking about it much. He would mutter a brief word or two about a move or a piece of business, and they would just do it straight away, calmly, without argument, without fuss; and it immediately looked right. Oh dear, they're all experts, I thought, alarmed. And when I got up to do my bits I could feel their calm eyes on me, watching me carefully.

The play was Jean Anouilh's *Antigone*, and I had the smallish part of Haemon, Antigone's lover. I wrote down my moves painstakingly so I wouldn't forget anything: I wanted to appear as businesslike and efficient as the others. I'm going to enjoy it here, I thought. After the rehearsal was over I went up to Geoffrey Ost and asked him the question which had been on my mind all morning: had he had a letter from Folkestone? From Mr Brough?

'Oh Peter,' he said, taking me aside so the others couldn't hear, 'I'm glad you've asked me. I didn't want to mention it in case you hadn't known about it. Yes, I have. A very odd letter indeed. It was written by someone who had obviously lost his temper. But I want you to know it hasn't altered my opinion of you, or influenced me one little bit. Nor will it.'

'Thank you,' I said gratefully.

After that I went to pieces. I couldn't do the part in *Antigone* or even remember the lines. I couldn't make the moves feel natural and I didn't know what to do with my hands. I was panicking and had no shield to protect me, no close chum yet in the company to whom I could run. (Close chums are so important. 'You need a chum,' said Paul Eddington the other day, 'in every company you are in, especially on tour.') The X-ray eyes of the others were watching me and I invented what they must be thinking.

Since then, like all actors and actresses, I suppose, I have panicked often: 'I will never ever ever be able to do this part.' But this was the first time it had happened to me in the professional theatre, and I didn't know what to do about it. I'll go back to my digs and slog, I thought: I'll work and work and work. Something will come. I won't go to bed tonight until I can do at least one of my scenes.

When I left the theatre and walked out into the cold, draughty streets of Sheffield I was suddenly homesick for Folkestone, where everything had been easy. I wished I'd never left, never given in my notice. Everything would have been all right then. I think I even wished I was back in the Army, where things had been easier still. The wretched thing about acting, I thought, is that it is so public. One is always on show. One is watched all the time, stared at by gimlet eyes. Writers, painters and composers are lucky: they do their important work in private. They will have their panics and their dud days, just like actors, but nobody else will see them. With us, the pressure of other people is constant and, when one's defences are down, can be withering. I wish I weren't so put off by other people, I thought: why does it happen?

Back in my room I re-arranged the chairs and tables to be like the ones on the stage. I propped the book up on the mantelpiece and went over to check it whenever I made a mistake. Each line, each move, each gesture I did over and over again, analysing them and planning them. I knew I would be nervous the following day so I had to have something really cast-iron worked out: only then, I thought, could I be sure that nerves and self-consciousness would not get in the way. And with every repetition the lines lost a little more meaning and the moves a little more spontaneity.

At rehearsal the following morning I was as wooden as I deserved to be and the words were just so much gibberish. 'I think we'd better go through your scenes this afternoon,' said Geoffrey. I knew at once I was in disgrace, for they *never* rehearsed in the afternoon. Barbara Clegg, who was Antigone, was none too pleased.

The lighting people wanted the stage for maintenance that afternoon, so we had to go into a little side room to practise. Barbara Clegg and I did our opening scene. Geoffrey said, 'Now just do it quietly, Peter, and think what you are saying. Don't charge at it so.' I tried to be obedient, but suddenly it all seemed so irresistibly stupid to me, so hushed – and in this silly little room with Geoffrey sitting on top of us – that I started to laugh. 'What are you laughing at, Peter? It's no laughing matter.'

'I know,' I said, 'I'm sorry. I didn't mean to laugh, I just couldn't help it.' Here I was, adding to the humiliation of having to work in the afternoon by giggling! And my first play in a new theatre, to boot! I couldn't believe it.

'Pull yourself together, then, and let's do it again.'

I managed to get half-way through and then started to giggle again. Barbara Clegg caught the infection and started too. Geoffrey was really annoyed. 'Stop it,' he said, very quietly, 'stop it. You are wasting my time.'

We tried to control ourselves but it was too late, the damage was done. The hysteria was growing rather than diminishing and it was impossible to stop.

'Go home,' said Geoffrey, wearily.

After the First Night I was not mentioned by the critics of either the *Sheffield Telegraph*, or the evening paper the *Star*. Everybody else was. And the play itself was well received. A few days later

Geoffrey asked me to see him in his office. Oh no, I thought: not the sack again!

'Don't worry,' he said, reading my white-faced thoughts as I went in, 'I only want to have a chat with you. Sit down.'

'I wish I could do this part,' I said, obsessed. 'But when I work on it it gets worse, not better. It's dreadful to be so bad in one's first play.'

'You're not nearly as bad as you think you are,' he said. 'Nobody's good all the time. It's one of the things about rep: you have parts which you can do easily and parts which will never seem comfortable. All you have to do is to say to yourself, well, if I'm not very good in this play, I'll be better in the next. And,' he said, leaning forward, confidentially, 'you're going to be very good in the next play: you're already more relaxed about it than you ever were or will be with *Antigone*. And don't forget, in a week and a half *Antigone* will be over, and you'll be on to the next play, and then the next.'

'Yes,' I said, relieved.

'Peter, I'm going to tell you something.' He got up and banged his pipe to empty it in the fireplace. He was a gentle, quiet man, and it showed in his face. He was really quite shy, and had a habit, which we all imitated, of patting his right elbow with his left hand while he talked. He wore sober sports jackets and grey flannels, and his brogue shoes were highly polished. He had a slight stoop, and walked heavily. His hair was always tidy. 'I think, and you must forgive me for bringing up the subject again, that you have been more disturbed than you realize by your unhappy leave-taking at Folkestone. It was obviously a very hard knock for you, and very unpleasant. It takes time to recover from things like that. When the big knocks come, like getting the sack, losing an important part, being out of work for an unconscionable time, or making enemies of people who had been friends, it is touch and go for a while between regaining enough confidence to carry on, and giving way altogether. At these times there is only a knife-edge between recovery and failure; and when there are rages, and people behave like savages to each other, failure becomes dangerously attractive.'

'I suppose so,' I said. 'I still feel depressed about it.'

'The real reason for his anger was that he wanted you to stay. And he wanted you to stay because he thought you were good. Nobody wants to lose a good actor. That was why he kept the job open for you when you joined up. He was looking after himself. We all are. We're not in it for charity.'

'I suppose so,' I said again.

'Well one thing I'll promise you: I won't be cross when you get another job. The only thing I ask is that if you are thinking of moving, you will take me into your confidence and tell me about it.'

I was feeling better by the minute as I listened to this wise, good man. 'Of course I will,' I said.

'Off you go,' he said. 'Your reputation preceded you. Peter Sallis thinks the world of you, otherwise he would not have recommended you. You'll soon be confident again. Work hard on each part, but not too hard.' He opened the door for me to go, and then said, 'What do you usually do on Sundays?'

'Well, work, really.'

'Don't. Take them off. Go out into the country. The Pennines near here are very beautiful, you know.'

'Yes, I know.'

'Try and enjoy the performance tonight. But remember: a play is only a play. Say to yourself: it's only a play . . . it doesn't matter all that much . . .'

I discovered, about a year later, that Geoffrey had been in grave doubts as to my ability. When he engaged me he had intended me to be Hamlet in the annual Shakespeare play. It was during the rehearsals for *Antigone* that he decided to look for someone else. I was relegated to Rosencrantz and the Second Gravedigger. How well he disguised his disappointment in me! Thank heavens I didn't know. But he was right. I had been more disturbed than I knew, and was still sprawling on the terrace outside Brough's office. It was to take me many months to recover my balance completely, and become the placid and composed actor Geoffrey wanted me to be.

Gradually I began to settle down and be less shy of the company; we were close enough: talking shop endlessly, as actors do wherever they are, and exclaiming fulsomely about each other's work. Paul Eddington was already a splendid comedian, and the funniest Faulkland, in *The Rivals*, I have ever seen. Patrick McGoohan went from strength to strength. He had had no training at all: he had lived in Sheffield all his life, and had applied for a job as an assistant stage manager. Geoffrey was impressed with him and took him on. He was soon the star of the company and gave powerful performances as Tanner in *Man and Superman* and Petruchio in *The Taming of the Shrew*. Peter Sallis was always good, with his dry wit and idiosyncratic speech, and Alan MacNaughton, Bernard Archard and many others gave notable performances. The women in the company never did as well as the men. Perhaps they were intimidated by us, I don't know; we were a formidable lot.

It was the ideal combination: this sparky, brilliant company set against the methodical, some said plodding, some said dull, character of Geoffrey Ost. The fireworks and technical expertise were ours; the long-term, peaceful, businesslike way of running the company was his. He expected us to offer vitality and clever characterization, and he often cast us adventurously: 'This'll stretch you a bit,' he would say, patting his elbow and grinning mischievously, when he presented us with a part which was wildly out of our range. 'Do you good,' he would say: 'It's just as important to play unsuitable parts as it is to play suitable ones, for they make you find new things in yourself . . . ooh, don't ask me what they will be, it's up to you. You'll have to fish around and find them.' Pat, pat.

'It's up to you,' he said. It was my first experience of do-it-yourself acting: but provided that the other actors are sympathetic, hard-working and talented, it can be surprisingly rewarding. There will be many misses, of course: but the hits can be startling because they haven't been interfered with.

'Well, at least you'll know when you leave here what you can do and what you can't.' And that, it seems to me, is the most important thing that can come out of being in a rep. That, and a growing sense of being at home on the stage. It is the sheer quantity of the work that matters: on an average day we would be on the stage in one play at ten o'clock in the morning, and still on it in another at ten o'clock at night.

The plays came and went. In one ear and out the other. My collection of reviews cut from local papers grew, and eventually filled a whole scrapbook. I had not looked at it for several years until the other day; and I found that I had forgotten some of the plays altogether. *Wilderness of Monkeys? Mrs Dane's Defence?* And what was *Treasure Hunt* all about? I would have denied I was ever in *The Little Foxes*, and sworn I'd never even heard of *Mr Gillie*. Geoffrey Ost's policy of not giving any more effort to each play than it needed, of working carefully but coolly, mornings only, certainly paid off: spirits remained high for the whole of a long season.

My own biggest personal success had, ironically, nothing to do with acting. Every Christmas the Playhouse had presented a musical play for children. We had given *The Silver Curlew* by Eleanor Farjeon for my first Christmas there, and I had been very taken by the songs and dances composed for it by Clifton Parker: based on English folk music, but brought up to date with a few wrong notes, the tunes were not immediately catchy, but once we had got used to their eccentricities they were unforgettable.

For the following Christmas Geoffrey chose *The Princess and the Swineherd*, a charming play by Nicholas Stuart Gray. It had no music, however, and Geoffrey was worried that the audiences might be disappointed if we gave them just a straight play.

'Shall I try and write some?' I piped up.

'Do you think you could?' said Geoffrey, taken aback and disbelieving.

'Well,' I said, 'I've written quite a few things over the years. Would you like to hear some of them?'

There was a fine grand piano in the auditorium, tucked away into a corner near the stage; and that afternoon, in the deserted theatre, I played what I could remember of my pieces to Geoffrey, while he hummed a little, patted his elbow, and paced about.

'Well, it's the right sort of music, Peter,' he said, when I had finished, 'and of course the splendid thing is you could play the piano for it too.'

'Be a nice break from acting,' I said, riskily.

'Do you think you can write songs, though?'

'Well, I never have done, but . . .'

'No . . .' and he thought for a while. 'I'll tell you what,' he said, plunging in, 'read the play and see what you think. I'll read it again and then we can exchange notes on how many songs and dances we need, and where they should go. And meanwhile I'll write to Nicholas Stuart Gray to ask his permission. If we're going to do it, we've got to get on with it. Sharpish.'

He was uncharacteristically excited. We were like schoolboys who had just thought up a huge practical joke to play on the headmaster, and we crept away surreptitiously, not quite saying to each other, 'Mum's the word!'

When I left the theatre that afternoon I was curiously elated. I didn't want to go back to the digs where I would be confined in a small room. I wanted to walk and walk, without stopping. I didn't care where I went or whether I knew where I was: all I wanted was the open air and a pavement under my feet.

I didn't doubt for a moment that I could write the music. I didn't doubt for a moment that it would be brilliant. I had all the confidence in the world. It doesn't matter where confidence comes from, as long as it comes. That afternoon it had come in abundance; and it had come because Geoffrey had treated me as an equal. He was my friend at last. I had never been able to use that word about him before, and now I could. I had never even had a drink with him in a pub before, and now I could. That afternoon my attitude to Geoffrey was turned turtle, and it has influenced my attitude to directors ever since. Good work comes when everybody is confident enough and relaxed enough to contribute without any inhibitions at all.

Permission for music was granted by Nicholas Stuart Gray, 'but only for the performances at Sheffield'. Geoffrey and I conferred, and agreed; and with Prokoviev, Vaughan Williams, Clifton Parker and all looking over my shoulder, I wrote my songs and dances and incidental music in five weeks flat. The biggest number was a market-day scene, when all the characters were on the stage singing different things at the same time.

The rehearsals went well. I was interviewed by the local press, and my photograph appeared in the *Sheffield Telegraph* over a large headline which read 'Actor Writes Songs for Christmas Play'.

The first performance was received with a fervour unknown in Sheffield, and when I took my bow at the end, the cheers were loud, and some of the audience stood. The papers were just as ecstatic. 'It was an enchanted evening,' wrote K.M.G. of the *Sheffield Telegraph*, 'and the chief magician was Peter Barkworth. Mr Barkworth is the composer of the incidental music, which he himself plays. Perhaps it is only one's fancy that he knows and loves his Delius; whatever the inspiration Mr Barkworth excelled all expectations and thoroughly deserved his ovation. "I was almost beginning to believe there is real magic," says the Princess somewhere in the midst of disillusion. Had she been sitting in the audience she would never have doubted the potent powers that belong to this production of Mr Gray's play.'

Nicholas Stuart Gray himself was not so happy. At a subsequent performance he sat with Paul Eddington at the back of the stalls, and during the market-day scene he turned to him and said, 'They've all gone mad.'

From then on I could do no wrong in the eyes of the critics of the *Telegraph* and the *Star*. And now that they had made a plate of my photograph it appeared week after week at the head of a review, often when I had quite a small part. I was asked to open bazaars and give prizes at schools. Now that I had another string to my bow I cut a more glamorous figure in the eyes of the theatre-goers of Sheffield. The surge of confidence spilled over into my acting, and in several performances I felt quite inspired. I became ambitious, wanting to take the next step and try to get into the Liverpool rep, whose reputation was second to none.

'A good move, Peter,' said Geoffrey when I told him. 'You've been here two years now and done well. From your point of view it's time for a change, I can see that. I don't want you to go, though; and my invitation to you to stay for a third year still stands.'

I went over to Liverpool to see Willard Stoker, who ran the rep. He told me he would let me know quite soon. He had to consult the board, he said; but he would give my application the most favourable attention, particularly as he had had a glowing letter about me from Geoffrey Ost.

'Thank you for writing to him,' I said to Geoffrey when I got back. He hadn't told me that he would.

'Well,' he said, quizzically, 'I remember your last change of job. I wanted this one to be different.'

He was a saint.

He also said, 'And I have to tell you, Peter, you are going to be wonderfully good in *Figure of Fun*. It's a pity Daphne Rye and Kenneth Carten are not going to see that. Ah well.' And he patted his elbow.

It was the event of the season: the visit to our theatre by Daphne Rye and Kenneth Carten. She was the casting director of H. M. Tennent Ltd, then the most powerful theatrical management in London, and he was a top agent working for Myron Selznick. Every summer they spent several weeks together visiting all the major repertory companies looking for new and exciting talent.

The play they were to see was *His Excellency*, by Dorothy and Campbell Christie, I didn't have much of a part and was mentioned only as one of the 'also rans' in the local papers. But I didn't care. I wasn't ready for London. I had set my heart on Liverpool, and on being as good as I could be in *Figure of Fun*. That day we had two run-throughs of it: one in the morning and one – rare occasion – in the afternoon. And during the afternoon there had been magic in the air. The play galloped away with itself, took off, became airborne. It doesn't happen often, but when it does it is the most glorious feeling in the world. I was in my seventh heaven, and that night gave a glittering performance in *His Excellency*.

Everybody else was frightfully nervous. I noticed it straight away. Ella Atkinson's face was twitching and her hands shook. Other people fluffed their lines and made silly mistakes. They were all so anxious to impress. I didn't give a fig. And I glittered. Everybody else's laughs were halved that night. Mine were doubled. It was the only good performance I gave.

After the show a message came round from Geoffrey, who had

sat with them: 'Miss Daphne Rye and Mr Kenneth Carten would be very pleased if Mr Peter Barkworth would join them for dinner at the Grand Hotel.'

The rest of the company put on a brave face. Oh, they had so hoped the message would be for them. They knew what dinner at the Grand Hotel meant.

They made an odd couple: Daphne Rye big-boned, soft-fleshed and bosomy, with full red lips which opened wide when she laughed, and Kenneth Carten emaciated, nervous, with a habit of clearing his throat every time he spoke. They both smoked incessantly, and drank fast.

Daphne Rye did most of the talking. 'Very good, you're very good,' she said. 'We enjoyed it, didn't we Kenneth?'

'Enormously,' he said, and cleared his throat.

'I shall have to confirm it with Binkie, but what I would like to offer you here and now, before we get too drunk, is a three-year contract with our firm. All that means really is that we guarantee to pay you a fairly modest salary, it will be, for three years. Obviously we shall try to find you as much work as possible in our plays. Do you like the sound ot it?'

'Oh yes,' I said, lost for anything else to say.

'Now Kenneth, do you want to talk to him before you get too drunk? He drinks a lot you know,' she added, *sotto voce*, and we all laughed.

He cleared his throat: 'I would like to represent you,' he said. 'I saw the RADA Public Show and admired you then, and I admired you even more tonight.'

'Geoffrey Ost tells us,' Daphne Rye barged in, 'that you are going to be especially good in your next play, so he has invited us to watch tomorrow morning's rehearsal.'

'Oh,' I said, 'how wonderful. How kind of him.'

'Nice man,' said Daphne Rye.

And that was it. That was the business done. I had two contracts. The one with H. M. Tennent was eventually extended to five years, and Kenneth Carten was my agent for twenty-six loyal years, until he retired in 1978.

We all got drunk. The evening became terribly ribald, with Daphne and Kenneth telling spicy stories about Binkie and Noel and Johnny and Vivien and Larry. They seemed to know all those famous people intimately, and as they never bothered with surnames I wasn't always sure who they were talking about. I can't remember anything particular about the rest of the evening, except there were a lot of jokes about the waiters, and which ones they fancied and which ones they didn't.

I can't remember how I got home.

At the beginning of *Figure of Fun*, Freddie, the part I played, is discovered standing on his head. When Daphne Rye and Kenneth Carten came to the rehearsal the following morning, I had to excuse myself from doing this, on account of an appalling hangover. They watched a run-through of Act I, said nice things, complained about their own headaches, and went off to catch their train to the next rep. That afternoon I wrote a letter to Willard Stoker, telling him what had happened. After I had posted it I went out of the town, climbed to the top of Hallam Moor, looked south across the Pennine hills, and said aloud, 'London, here I come!'

Going Downhill

My first play in London under the H. M. Tennent banner was *Letter from Paris*, an adaptation by Dodie Smith of Henry James's novel *The Reverberator*. In the cast were Brenda Bruce, Nicholas Hannen, Maxine Audley, Marjorie Stewart, Nicholas Phipps, Eliot Makeham, Jessie Evans and Scott McKay, and it was directed by Peter Glenville. After a tour we opened at the Aldwych Theatre on Friday 10 October 1952, and at the end of the performance we were booed by a vociferous gallery.

We took too many curtain calls, and each time we bowed to the applauding stalls, the boos from the gallery got louder. Harold Hobson commented the following Sunday: 'I am continually surprised at the insensitiveness of West End managements which, during recent years, by taking up the curtain oftener than the real feeling of the house justifies, have frequently subjected their players to a cruel ordeal. Surely a management as able as that presenting *Letter from Paris* has someone upon its staff capable of assessing the judgment of the audience accurately enough not to botch this delicate and important matter of curtain calls?'

Nowadays, thank goodness, there is a saner attitude to curtain calls, or more usually to switch-the-lights-on-and-off-as-abruptly-as-you-can calls, the general belief rightly being that too few is better than too many. But for us the twelve or so calls we took that

As Archie Fellowes in The Shop at Sly Corner.

The disastrous Love in Idleness. *Me with a pipe and Elizabeth Addyman, Peter Walter and Diana Johnson.*

(Lambert Weston & Son Ltd)

My first television part, with Barbara Jefford.

(A. John Cura)

A haloed second lieutenant in the Royal Artillery.
(Barker Longson)

The Leas Pavilion, Folkestone.

Geoffrey Ost.

night marked the end of two and a half hours of muted laughter and frequent signs of restlessness. A First Night audience is unlike any other: an uncomfortable mixture of friends, relations, critics, celebrities and theatre buffs, all rather nervously anxious to assess accurately the merits and demerits of the play and its performers. This desire for accuracy is reflected in the laughs, the silences and, at the end, the applause – all of which seem curiously regulated, as though everyone there is awarding marks out of ten. The actors are invariably acutely nervous; and the nerves are not the natural ones of a true first performance, because that will have happened on tour or at a preview: they are nerves compounded of fright, of worry about being on form in front of this important and clinical audience, and of anxiety as to what the notices will be like the following day. There may well be some actors who actually enjoy the prospect of a First Night in London, but I have yet to meet one.

What was particularly dispiriting about the First Night of *Letter from Paris* was that it followed a rapturous reception from the Edinburgh audience we had played to the previous Saturday. 'What a wonderful send-off!' we said to each other as we packed up our make-up and folded our clothes ready for London: 'If it goes anything like that next Friday, we'll have nothing to worry about.'

This contrast between a final Saturday night on tour and the subsequent opening night in London was even more marked in several other plays I was to be in, the most alarming being a revival of Shaw's *Misalliance* in 1956, which was received with cheers and stamping in Cambridge, and almost total disbelieving silence at the Lyric, Hammersmith, until Donald Pleasence went on and got ten out of ten. The rest of us got nought. When the curtain came down for the interval Roger Livesey shook his fist towards the audience and said, 'Bastards! bastards!' When a play goes so much less well at a First Night the actors lose their confidence: they cannot help but compare each reaction, moment by moment, with what they have known before. They feel stodgy and disliked, and fervently wish the whole thing over. It's not the end of the world, but it feels like it.

We were a melancholy troupe as we traipsed back to our dressing-rooms after the first performance of *Letter from Paris*. There was the usual blah as friends flocked round: 'Well done, well done, congratulations, marvellous, wonderful, most enjoyable, beautiful performance, welcome to London, very good, an auspicious debut, fine, extraordinarily good; the people in the gods were fools; didn't know a good thing when they saw one; rabble; stupid; saw one or two of them, louts; anyway it wasn't you they were booing, it was the play; don't worry, don't worry, don't worry . . .'

It was all so insistent, in my dressing-room and later over dinner at the Caprice, that I began to forget about my doubts and dreads and to believe instead that I had indeed scored a major personal triumph in a hugely successful play.

It was not true. The notices the following morning were pleasant and mild and pointed out faults and virtues in about equal measure. I received some nice mentions – 'excellent', 'most satisfactory', 'agreeable', 'pleasant', 'admirable' – but had obviously not set the world on fire, or taken London by the storm I had secretly predicted for myself. Subsequently we had very poor houses, and the play was withdrawn after three weeks. I was glad: it had been miserable doing it night after night to a handful of people, with hardly any reaction and with thin applause. I didn't know it would be the last time I was to have a leading role in London for twenty years.

My greatest source of pleasure while I was in *Letter from Paris* was a growing friendship with Dodie Smith. She seemed more concerned that my first play in London was a flop and that I might lose confidence thereby than about her own lack of success with it. She talked a lot about it to me, apportioning praise and blame to herself, the cast, the director and the designer, and I was happy to be taken into her confidence.

She was a small, white-faced woman with straight dark hair drawn tightly back over her ears. Her features were a little too sensual to say she looked like a nun, but there was a withdrawn air about her, as though she was in part thinking about what she was saying, but in part remembering some far-off occurrence which would not leave her. She was delicate, almost frail, even then. She spoke softly and quickly and kept still as she did so.

What I admired most about her, and still do, was that as well as being compassionate and generous she was quite surprisingly tough. At least it surprised *me*. She stood up for what she wanted and said what she believed in, and wouldn't give an inch when other people made her cross or dispirited. It was the first time I had seen such firmness of purpose in a friend, and it pointed out to me my own vacillations: how easily I was thrown when people were unpleasant, and how much I capitulated when I wanted to please. I don't think I made any resolutions then about trying to be tougher, but I saw how desirable it was. 'You should stick to your guns, Peter, when you know you are right,' she said, when I questioned her about it. 'I admire people who say what they mean, have the courage of their convictions, and don't abandon them just to keep the peace.'

Young actors and actresses nowadays seem to me to be much more forthright and sure than I was: more honest and able to defend themselves. It is something to do with the general flavour of the time, I suppose: the authority of parents, teachers and employers is continually questioned, and everybody cries out for democracy and freedom and doing their own thing. Task-masters and tyrants are out. Or nearly; not quite. But it's better now. A young actress said to me recently, praising Michael Blakemore, the director of the play she was rehearsing, 'It is so good to be working with someone who gives you help and love in equal proportions. I just collapse when a director is horrid.' Oh, join the gang, I thought, but didn't say.

One night, after the show, Dodie entertained me to supper in the sitting-room of her suite at the Ritz. It was the first time I had ever eaten so grandly in private, and when the two waiters wheeled in the table and arranged our chairs and flicked our napkins at us I was terribly impressed. There was wine on ice, and hot soup which they served and cleared away, and then they left us with a cold collation. I was relieved when they had gone. Now we could really talk.

'Help yourself to the wine, dear,' she said. 'I don't want any more.'

'This is wonderful,' I said, 'but it must be frightfully expensive here, isn't it?'

'Yes it is quite. I suppose I'm absurdly extravagant, but I love it.'

'Do you mind telling me how much it is?'

'Not at all. It's seven pounds a night.'

'Seven pounds a night!' I exclaimed. It was unheard of: 'That's forty-nine pounds a week!'

'That's right,' she said.

'What do you get for that?'

'Oh, just the suite.'

'No food?'

'Oh no.'

I couldn't believe it. 'You must be very rich,' I said.

'Well,' she said, in her matter-of-fact way, 'yes. I'm what you would call well-to-do, I suppose. But it wasn't always so. When I left RADA and couldn't find work as an actress, I was down and out. Desperate. Eventually I got a job as a sales assistant at Heal's in Tottenham Court Road for thirteen pounds a month. Thirteen pounds plus one per cent commission on what I sold.'

I have always enjoyed talking about money and have never subscribed to the view that to do so is to be socially gauche. Dodie enjoyed it too, and what she was to tell me that night has influenced me ever since.

'I think money should be fun,' she said. 'I have always thought so, even when I was very poor. When I was an actress there was no unemployment pay, you know. And of course no pay for rehearsals. Compared to today it was monstrous. But I used to enjoy working out what I could afford and what I couldn't. I made lists and predictions. I moved into a room which was over a bakery and was therefore quite warm so I could save on electricity. That meant that occasionally I could afford a nicer meal or a new pair of stockings.' It was strange to hear her talk about poverty in such opulent surroundings. 'I tried never to stint on clothes,' she continued. 'And when I wasn't an actress any more I would still dress quite carefully, and wear what I thought was appropriate for meeting people or for my job at Heal's. You know, Peter, you should never throw anything away. You never know when it'll come in useful. Actors should have large wardrobes; if it's a modern play it's much better to wear your own things if you can . . . especially if they're supposed to be old clothes. Hired things rarely look lived in.'

'Yes,' I said.

'But the most important thing,' she said, getting back to the subject of money, 'is to save a little every week. It's surprising how quickly it grows. Do you save?'

'Well I can't in London,' I said, 'because it's so expensive here. But I did in Sheffield.'

'How much?'

'Oh well,' I said, reeling slightly from the direct questions and drink, 'er . . . a pound a week.'

'Regularly?'

'Yes. Well, nearly. The only way I could make sure it was

regular was to put it in the bank the minute I was paid. If I left it till the end of the week I'd spend it.'

'That's right,' she said, 'that's the way to do it. And it's fun. It gives even missing a meal a purpose. Anyway, eventually I had saved up enough for a holiday in Switzerland. And it was there that I got the idea for *Autumn Crocus*. It was my first play for the professional theatre.'

'Was it a huge success straight away?' I asked.

'Oh yes,' she said, 'it started me off. So you see . . .'

There was a silence for a moment, while she thought about it.

'What did you think of me before you met me?' she asked suddenly.

'Ooh! Well, a sort of rich man's Esther McCracken.'

She laughed. 'That's not bad. Yes, I originated the idea of gentle plays about families of the time . . . not great stories, but believable and natural characters and dialogue in believable and natural situations. Esther McCracken did the same after me . . .' and she drifted into silence again, thinking of her past successes, comparing them with the play we were both so heavily involved in. 'Ah well,' she said.

She was the most peaceful companion I have ever known, and I thought so again the other day when I visited her at her beautiful thatched house in Finchingfield in Essex. She is still inquiring and interested as she always was. And as active: 'Oh yes, I write every day. And I read a little from Mary Baker Eddy every day too.' (She describes herself as a vague Christian Scientist.) 'It's lovely to see you on television,' she said, 'for we never go out now. I don't like to. It's all so noisy and awkward. I haven't seen a play for years. I like to be here. It's so quiet. It's mostly autobiography I'm doing now. Haven't got up to you yet,' she said, and we all laughed. We'd gone for afternoon tea, and we sat in her cream-coloured drawing-room, and talked about books and work and catching up with news until it started to get dark. She was tired so we left quite quickly. She stood on the porch to wave us goodbye, and we didn't talk at all on the way home . . .

It was Coronation Year, 1953, and the H. M. Tennent empire dominated the London theatre more powerfully than ever: the Lunts were in *Quadrille*, Edith Evans and Sybil Thorndike in *Waters of the Moon*, Ralph Richardson in *The White Carnation*, and there was a John Gielgud season at the Lyric, Hammersmith; *The Deep Blue Sea* was at the Duchess, *Seagulls Over Sorrento* at the Apollo, *The Little Hut* at the Lyric; and they were joined in February by a revival of *A Woman of No Importance* at the Savoy. Oscar Wilde's play had been 'specially adapted' by Paul Dehn, the lavish settings and costumes were by Loudon Sainthill, the director was the discreet and charming Michael Benthall, and in the cast were Clive Brook, Nora Swinburne, Athene Seyler, Jean Cadell, Isabel Jeans, Aubrey Mather, William Mervyn and Frances Hyland. My part was Gerald Arbuthnot. We had a two-week try-out at the Theatre Royal, Brighton, and although our First Night in London received mixed notices, there was sufficient use of words like 'dazzling', 'sumptuous', 'triumphant' and 'magnificent' to give the management plenty of quotations for advertisements and hoardings. It looked like a glittering success; but, alas, all that glisters is not gold, and beneath the wit and the shine and the glamour there were demons at work, destroying much of the pleasure and making the six-month run a very unnerving experience indeed.

It may seem churlish, after all this time, to write about turbulences within a company. It could be argued that the theatre is what it is because the public seldom knows anything about what goes on back-stage; and this is just as well: the theatre is a show-place, and the only thing that matters is the play. If the audience knew anything about the affairs, animosities and worries among the performers, the play would be destroyed for them and they would not be able to concentrate on it. Fact would get in the way of fiction. It still feels strange to me when I go back-stage after having enjoyed a play and having been taken in by it to hear actors' stories about rows and awkwardnesses, for they seem irrelevant and in danger of spoiling the experience of the play. Nevertheless, of course it's nice to have news!

But as I am attempting here to give an honest account of my experiences, good and bad, and the effect they had on my confidence and ability, I feel bound to say just a bit about what went on back-stage, for it was profoundly disturbing.

Clive Brook soon revealed to us all at rehearsals that he was worried about having accepted his part of Lord Illingworth. 'Oh, I can't do it. I can't do it,' he said pathetically one early day, and we all felt sorry for him. He was a proud man, and disliked growing older. It infuriated him that he found the part so difficult to learn; and he was having trouble with some new artificial teeth, which caused his hitherto incisive delivery to become blurred and pedantic and hard to hear. He hated his balding head and often kept his hat on at rehearsals, a substitute for the toupee he invariably wore for performances. The rehearsals tired him and we could see he was beginning to panic. He stalked about, worrying over every move, and arguing a lot. He was jealous of the way some of the women in the cast were progressing in their roles, finding it much easier than he to learn the lines and find the style. Isabel Jeans and Athene Seyler in particular were romping home. He took me aside one day and said. 'Never act in a play where the women have the best parts! They will destroy you. Let's stick together, you and me!'

And I admired him. I admired his guts, and the effort he put into learning the lines and being as elegant and dapper as he could. It was costing him too much, though, and one day he exploded.

It was the most dreadful row I have ever heard. A triviality sparked it off: one of Isabel Jeans's moves. He started to shout at her – 'Oh no you don't, Miss bloody Jeans' – and became a mountain of temper; when he'd said all he wanted to say to her and to the rest of us, he stalked off the stage declaring he would resign from the play. Athene Seyler rushed into the wings after him, and, after what seemed like hours of urgent muttering, eventually coaxed him back. But nobody was to forget all that shouting. Or forgive it. All the warmth Michael Benthall had given to us was wasted, and everybody realized they just had to look after their own performances or sink. It was a pity, for the company was filled with pleasant and talented people who, in other circumstances, would have delighted in being in a play together.

Cliques formed, and we whispered in corners. For Clive Brook it became a grim endurance test.

When we opened at Brighton he was given a poor review in the *Evening Argus* while Isabel Jeans got the one rave: 'From a company as excellent as this, it is difficult to single out any one person, but by a narrow margin the honours must go to Isabel Jeans as Mrs Allonby. Her liquid gold voice wraps itself caressingly around those Wilde epigrams, adding to them a sharper edge, a deeper meaning. She is the woman of the world, *par excellence*.' The women regarded this as a vindication of all they had been through, while poor Clive Brook was humiliated beyond endurance. Every day he threatened to walk out of the production and he kept his bags permanently packed.

I can't remember much about the rest of the time in Brighton except that it rained incessantly. When we weren't in the theatre, Frances Hyland and I just skulked about, not daring to speak much. 'It doesn't make it any easier to do, does it?' she said, after a performance one night. 'There's a lot of daring in acting, and if you don't dare speak in everyday life, you feel inhibited when you get on the stage, because you're facing the same people.'

There was little laughter backstage. This is unusual among actors, for we tend to laugh a lot. Athene Seyler says in her book *The Craft of Comedy* that she likes to laugh in her dressing-room before going on stage: it helps her feel scintillating and witty. She didn't get much opportunity for that in Brighton. Low spirits are dreadfully damaging to a company: they make everybody feel dull and uncertain.

The notices in London were broadly like the one in the *Argus*, and Clive Brook became resigned to his lack of success. On the First Night, in the wings, he said to me, 'Treat the audience as cabbages, boy! They are nothing. If they were anything, they would be up here doing it instead of us. They are nothing. They are cabbages.' It was just to keep himself going. He still flared up from time to time, though, and once he got so cross with Nora Swinburne that he stamped his foot and left the stage before the scene was over. Nora was quite overcome with horror, and when they next met on the stage, she completely forgot her first line and whispered plaintively instead, 'What have I done?'

I was to see more examples of extreme temperament in other plays in the fifties and it made me resolve that if ever I were to be in a leading position in a company, which seemed growingly unlikely, I would make it my first task to help keep the atmosphere as light-hearted and unself-indulgent as possible: good work flourishes only in friendly surroundings, and there is no point in allowing harshness to dominate. Clive Brook knew the rest of the company were against him and it did his performance no good at all. It would not have cost him much to take us into his confidence and apologize, but he never did, and he was the one to suffer.

Temperamental displays have decreased enormously with the new generation of actors. In fact in the last ten years I have seen none at all. I have been wondering why this is so. Could it be that the style of acting has changed since the fifties, and with it the demands made on the stars? There is a down-to-earth reality required by most modern plays, and encouraged by our great contemporary directors; and the advent of television has also contributed to a desire among actors to be truthful and real at all costs, and to bring a new ordinariness to their characterizations. It was not like that in the fifties. Productions of well-made plays were spotless and smooth, with everybody moving elegantly around sofas and drinks tables. Clothes were never allowed to be creased, and make-up was worn by the men as well as the women. The theatre was the place for glamour and high style. Attempts at truth and reality were certainly made, but the stars were expected to shine and were worshipped like gods. (On the tour of *The Sleeping Prince* mounted police were needed to control the crowds waiting at stage doors just to catch a glimpse of Vivien Leigh and Laurence Olivier.) They were expected to be beautiful, like royalty and the stars of the ballet, and they were. I don't think I have ever seen or heard anything as beautiful as Edith Evans in *Daphne Laureola*. She caressed James Bridie's sentences and turned them into gold. As Ruth Ellis said about another of her performances, 'In her speaking, rhythm and phrase have a new compelling power, climbing to new beauty, illuminating the play until it is "a feasting presence full of light".'

Dame Edith and many other stars stretched themselves like ballet dancers stretch their bodies and opera singers their voices. They were single-minded about their art. Dame Edith said to me once, 'I have only one aim in life: to make myself a better actress.'

For us lesser mortals, though, they were uncomfortable acting partners: very demanding, full of rules. I was in eight plays in the fifties, and there was invariably a tension between the stars and their supporting actors, and childish tantrums seemed part and parcel of what we were to expect.

I think it was generally agreed that Nora Swinburne, Frances

Hyland and I gave sensitive and truthful performances of the three rather awful 'goodies' in A *Woman of No Importance*, though we were helped by Paul Dehn's excision of the worst of the melodramatic lines. At least we rarely got laughs in the wrong place, and that was regarded as a triumph. (Everybody else, except Clive Brook, got a lot of laughs in the right place and that was regarded as a triumph too.)

So I was looking forward to what promised to be a long run. How pleasant, I thought, to go in to a smart West End theatre every night to give another performance of a smart West End play. And how equally pleasant, I thought, to have so much free time during the day: time for long lie-ins in the mornings and lunches with friends; time for other people's matinées and more films than usual; time for long walks round Sevenoaks on nice days, and art galleries when it rained. How pleased I was with the prospect: I was a proper London juvenile at last!

Unhappily demons were at work in my own mind as well as within the company, and I was finding it harder and harder to perform my part well. The old bugbear of self-consciousness was rearing its head in a strange new form. Naively I had thought that as the run of the play progressed everything would get easier and better. But it wasn't like that at all.

The trouble with being in a long run, which makes it so fascinating and difficult an exercise, is that you know the play too well. You know every detail, not only of your own performance, but of everybody else's. Every line, every thought, every move, every gesture has been decided upon and practised, chewed over at home and talked about in rehearsal. And what is expected of you in performance is that you repeat the lines and the actions with as much accuracy and life as possible.

But when the play has been on for some months it is all too easy to allow concentration to wander. You don't need the whole of your mind to be devoted to the performance. You can do the proverbial laundry-lists in your head, and plan the shopping for tomorrow morning. Or if you are like I was in those far-off days, and inclined to be self-conscious anyway, you can just be self-conscious. The spare mind which I didn't need for the play went floating out into the audience, turned and, as though attaching itself to a person sitting out there, stared back at me, watching critically every move, every stance, every gesture and every facial expression.

My performance, which I think had always been a little wooden – partly on account of the manners of the period – became stiff as iron. Gestures became difficult to do where they had once been easy, and my legs felt heavy, like artificial ones. Daphne Rye came unexpectedly to a matinée and said afterwards to someone else in the company, 'What has happened to Peter Barkworth? And what about all that ghastly smiling?' This was reported to me verbatim the same evening, just before I went on stage, and the words 'ghastly smiling' haunted me for months. I developed a terrible inhibition about it, like people sometimes do when they pose for still photographs, and my lips would become dry like parchment. I had to smother them with lip-salve before each entrance. I felt mortified and couldn't shake off my inhibitions. I didn't know what to do about them, so eventually I decided to go and ask Athene Seyler what she thought.

'Dear boy,' she said, after I had blurted it all out to her, 'I'm sorry to hear all this, because it must take all enjoyment out of your acting, and enjoyment is such an important thing. Really, you know, if you don't enjoy it, there's not much point in doing it, is there? You might just as well find something else to do!'

'I often think that,' I said.

'Now, now,' she said. 'First of all, I have to tell you, you have surprised me by what you have told me. I didn't think you were nearly as self-conscious as you say you are. And that means it doesn't show. It doesn't show,' she repeated. I did not believe her, but it was nice to hear, and whether she was speaking the truth or not, it was the best thing she could have said. 'However,' she continued, 'try to think, when you are talking and listening on the stage, not about yourself, but about the other people. About the rest of us. And think anything, it doesn't matter. Have a good look at Clive's toupee and think about that. You'll be able to think about that for some time!' She laughed to her image in her dressing-room mirror: she was making herself up for that evening's performance. 'Think of Nora and what a nice woman she is, and think of how much you like dear little Frances Hyland. Think lots of things about us all.'

'Thank you very much,' I said, and made for the door.

'Peter dear boy,' she said, and I turned, 'you are very good in this play. It's not the easiest of parts, you know, and you do it with such truth and such modern reality . . . I honestly cannot imagine the part being played better by any other young actor, because what you do is right. All three of you are good. Oh I know the rest of us get far more reward from the audience, because they laugh at us, but you get their admiration, for you bring off a most difficult task. I couldn't begin to do it myself.'

After the performance was over and we had taken our curtain-calls she said, , 'Did you enjoy it a little more tonight?'

'Oh yes,' I said. 'Thank you.'

'You are terribly good in it,' she whispered, furtively, 'I was watching you.'

That was the beginning of a long slow haul out of the trough of despondency into which I had so unexpectedly fallen. There were to be further slithers back into it, but at any rate I had been given as sound a piece of advice as I had ever received, on which I could lean in the future. Of course I did my level best to conceal my insecurities from both audiences and friends; and was, as Athene Seyler said, largely successful. I record them here only to show they existed, as I believe they do in many different, and equally successfully concealed, guises in most actors at some time in their lives. We are like pressure cookers: there's a lot of steam and turbulence and tension and panic, but the lid is firmly on.

Most actors incline to self-consciousness in some degree. It goes with the job, it seems, and we all have to learn how to cope with it and, hopefully, how to use it to our advantage, as it makes us more acutely aware of the myriads of activities, large and small, that go on in our minds and our bodies. In his book *An Actor Prepares*, Stanislavski wrote: 'In ordinary life you walk and sit and talk and look, but on the stage you lose all these faculties. You feel the closeness of the public and you say to yourself, "Why are they looking at me?" That is why it is necessary to correct ourselves and learn again how to walk, move about, sit or lie down. It is essential to re-educate ourselves to look and see, on the stage, to listen and to hear.'

That is it. Some time or other, sooner or later, that re-education has to happen. And then we know what walking is and what talking is, and listening. When we know these things, they will not let us down and we can concentrate again, not on ourselves, but on the other people and our intentions and attitudes towards them.

There is no substitute for detail. We need to carry on to the stage a mind brimming with ideas, with knowledge of the story of the play and the characters involved. What I omitted to do, in my early days, was to give myself enough to think about. It is only a comparatively empty mind that yields to self-consciousness.

Another demon was beginning to loom, though: I was becoming superstitious. And not just over the well known hazards (such as walking under ladders, quoting *Macbeth* or whistling in the dressing-room, using a new stick of greasepaint on a First Night), but over home-made ones as well. I invented the most impossible puzzles to solve on my bus journey from St John's Wood, where I then lived, to the theatre. If I hadn't solved them by the time I got off the bus, that would mean I would give a bad performance. One of the puzzles was that I had to think of at least five people whose Christian names and surnames began with the two letters at the bottom of the bus ticket. I had between Abbey Road and Trafalgar Square to do it; but when the two letters were TZ or QO I knew I hadn't a hope. A bad performance did not always result from such failures, I realized that: but the fear was real enough.

I had a superstition, too, about always taking the same route to the theatre. I would get off at the same bus stop, walk along the same side of the Strand, go down the little alleyway by the Coal Hole pub, turn left at the bottom of the steps and into the stage door. I never admitted it to anyone; and if I had gone out to tea after a matinée with someone in the company, then had had a walk by the river and approached the stage door from the Embankment, I would make a pretence of going as far as my dressing-room but not close the door, and then when I thought the coast was clear I would go out again up to the Strand and walk back by the necessary route.

I am told this superstition is quite common. But how stupid it all seems to me now! And I am sure to you too, as you read this. How can our common sense, which we like to think we all have in such large measure, be so cast aside in favour of demons? Where do they come from? How do they take hold? They come sometimes in such pernicious forms: not only in absurdities like superstition and suspicion, but, more dangerously and commonly I suppose, in reliance on cigarettes or drugs or drink. It is dreadful to see these things, which used in moderation can give such pleasure, take control of people, and rule and wreck their lives.

A *Woman of No Importance* came to an end. Tennent's had no part for me, so they asked me to be a non-speaking footman in *The Sleeping Prince*. From leading man to a walk-on in one year flat, I thought despondently, and tried to look the other way. I did not like the way things were going.

It was good to watch the Oliviers at work, though: Vivien Leigh, pretty and graceful, her voice clear as a bell, and everything about her so dainty and right for the part, and Laurence Olivier with his apparently limitless resources of vocal colours and inventive ideas. He directed the play as well as acting in it, and at early rehearsals, for the scenes he wasn't in, he would sit behind a desk, with his back to the curtain, and direct from there. Most days he was nice and jolly, and both he and Vivien Leigh were extraordinarily generous to the company, but sometimes he was curiously morose, and once he was cross with Martita Hunt for arriving late.

'Where's Marty?' he had said to Diana Boddington, the stage manager.

'I'll ring her, shall I?' said Diana.

Not a word was spoken by anybody while she was away telephoning. We all sat round the bare stage of the Phoenix Theatre, on uncomfortable wooden benches or on the iron steps of a spiral staircase which led up to the flies.

Diana came back, red in the face. 'There's no reply,' she said, 'so I assume she's left home.'

'Then we will wait for her,' said Sir Laurence, sitting behind his desk. He put his head in his hands and waited. The silence was intense. Nobody dared speak. Jeremy Spenser and I and some of the others caught each other's eyes and started to giggle.

'It's no laughing matter,' said Sir Laurence. We reverted to a ghastly silence and tried not to look at each other and to think of other things. After twenty or so minutes Martita Hunt arrived, breathless with apologies which he received in silence. When she had finished he just said, 'Yes, well . . .' and the rehearsal continued.

But the sight of Sir Laurence, so lonely and forlorn, sitting

motionless behind his desk for such a long time, had riveted itself
into my mind and became the basis of a recurring nightmare. I
would dream I was alone on the stage of a large theatre,
performing my part in a play which I had not even read.
Sometimes the play became an opera which I did not know either,
so I had to make up the music as well as the words. In the
auditorium all the seats had been taken out and in their places
were rows and rows of desks: in the stalls, in the dress circle and
the upper circle. And behind each desk sat Laurence Olivier.

The play opened its pre-London tour in Manchester, so there
was quite a bit about me in the papers. Local boy makes good. I
couldn't see that I was making much good in this particular play in
which I had so little to do, but of course it was because I was 'with'
Laurence Olivier and Vivien Leigh, two of the most glamorous
names in the whole of show business, and to be 'with' them meant
that I was on my way to the top. I was quite glad to read all this, for
it was face-saving. I started to adopt the 'with' myself. 'Oh yes,' I
would say to old schoolfriends, 'I am appearing at the Opera
House, actually, in Rattigan's *The Sleeping Prince*, with Laurence
Olivier and Vivien Leigh.' I knew there was a danger of its
sounding as if I was co-starring with them, but I didn't mind,
and if my hearers were silly enough to think that, so much the
better.

This name-dropping is what many people resort to when they
have little to do in a production. 'Oh yes,' they say, 'of course
when I was in *Where Eagles Dare* with Richard Burton and Clint
Eastwood we were having lunch one day and . . .' I always think
it's funny.

I realized, however, that I was rather enjoying having a
diminished responsibility. It had been nice not to have any lines
to learn, and not to get in a state about my performance half-way
through rehearsals when everybody is inclined to think they will
never be able to do it. It was nice, too, to go to the theatre without

apprehension and with no nerves at all; it didn't matter any more if I was tired after a late party the night before. I could regard the tour as a holiday, and go for long walks in the autumn countryside without feeling guilty. There was time for reading and listening to music and going to art galleries. Oh, I thought, there are many worse occupations than touring major English cities with a popular play, and having no responsibility whatsoever, and being paid for it.

I have noticed that I have always been happiest when I have had either nothing to do or a lot. It is the in-between times that are the hardest to cope with. It is not only that a leading role is usually easier to play than a supporting one, on account of being more rounded, better written, more interesting and offering greater opportunities, but that it carries with it, necessarily, a position of authority within the company. A supporting actor has to be obedient; a leading actor can call the tune. Leading actors are expected to be generous and warm-hearted towards the supporting cast, to be welcoming and concerned, to give presents and parties, and this, to me, is all part of the attraction.

The only cloud over my idle blue-sky days in *The Sleeping Prince* was that I had to understudy both Richard Wattis and Jeremy Spenser. I was not nearly old enough for Richard Wattis's part, and far too old for Jeremy Spenser's: a sixteen-year-old boy king. I used to dread the weekly understudy rehearsal, held on the morning of the mid-week matinée day, for I felt inadequate in both parts.

Understudy rehearsals are invariably dreary and can be quite soul-destroying. To go through the lines and moves of somebody else's part at ten o'clock in the morning, with the stage manager holding the book and everybody being curiously uncertain as to what the principal actors do during the performances, is a richly unrewarding experience.

'No, I'm sure she hands him the sandwich on *that* line.'

'No she doesn't. I saw it last night. She doesn't hand him a sandwich at all. He just takes one.'

'Well then she's changed it.'

'No, she never handed him a sandwich.'

'She did, I remember.'

'Well she didn't last night.'

'Oh well, I'll watch it this afternoon.'

Only the working light is on and everybody looks pale and ghastly. Voices have a morning thickness. Everybody knows the play to distraction: they sat in the stalls during the original rehearsals and hear it every night over the tannoy. They know it so well it has become meaningless, and the understudy rehearsals are merely a matter of getting through the lines with some sort of accuracy and being more or less in the right place. Cleaners are at work in the auditorium, tipping up the seats and hoovering. 'Can we have a little quiet please,' yells the stage manager. The hoovering stops for a time and dusting and polishing takes place. 'Thank you,' yells the stage manager. But now there are bar noises: empties are being thrown into cardboard cases, and new deliveries unpacked. 'Can we have some quiet please!' yells the stage manager again. 'Sorry, we've got to do this *now*,' someone unseen yells back. 'Well close the bloody door then!' The door is shut with a loud bang.

And so on. Week after week. The actors get through the play somehow, riding gamely over the difficulties of talking to themselves if they understudy more than one part, and go off to lunch at a nearby café, moaning to each other until it is time to come back for the matinée.

At the end of the year I auditioned five times for the part of Stefan in *The Dark is Light Enough* by Christopher Fry. When eventually Peter Brook said, 'It's yours', I was so dazed with gratitude that it did not occur to me that he must have had grave doubts as to my ability and rightness for the part, and had probably been talked into having me by the Tennent management. During the five weeks of rehearsals I did my best and I liked the part greatly, but I could establish no rapport with Peter Brook, nor he with me, and we remained distant and unfriendly. It was a deep, difficult play. Edith Evans and James Donald were enormously demanding of his attention and time, and to the rest of us he spoke only briefly. This made his occasional criticisms seem harsher than they were, for they were not cushioned by encouragement and praise.

When we arrived in Edinburgh where we opened in February 1954, we saw for the first time the elaborate and grandiose sets designed by Oliver Messel. The one for the first act, described in the script as 'a room and a great staircase', had a smallish window at the back, and it had to be snowing outside. The snow effect looked very good. There were two sacks filled with a white powder behind either side of the window, and two men threw shovelfuls of the stuff up in the air to be blown about by two electric fans. We all agreed that the whirling and swirling of the snow was very convincing indeed. Little did we imagine the havoc it was to cause.

The window had no glass or cellophane or anything in it, and during the first performance I was horrified to see a cloud of minute white particles gradually float in through the window, across the stage and out towards the audience. Edith Evans didn't know what was happening, but had to keep clearing her throat. I coughed several times, but that was nothing to the coughing that started in the audience as the cloud seeped right through the theatre. It was a barrage of coughing: coughing such as I had never heard; and it drowned the end of the act.

After the interval James Donald, Frances Hyland and I were waiting in the wings for the curtain to go up on Act II, in which, thank goodness, there was no snow. Peter Brook, white-faced with anger, stormed up to us and said, 'For God's sake speak up!

You cannot be heard. You are all inaudible. You are killing the play.'

I decided then and there to speak my mind. 'It's that bloody snow,' I said. 'There was a cloud of little white particles in the air. I saw it. I could hardly speak for the stuff. And that's why the audience is coughing too: it's got into all their throats.'

'Rubbish,' said Peter Brook. 'The audience is coughing because they are bored. They are bored because they can't hear. You are all too quiet – you especially, Peter – so for God's sake speak up!'

'We can't,' I persisted, surprising myself. 'As long as that snow stays, we can't.'

'Rubbish,' he repeated, and left us to go round the dressing-rooms.

The next day the Edinburgh papers were extremely scathing about the play and its performance, and that night a thin house coughed as mercilessly as the first had done. A meeting of the company was called for Wednesday morning at ten o'clock.

We were a subdued lot as we sat in a semicircle on the stage, waiting for Peter Brook and Christopher Fry to arrive. Edith Evans looked unhappy and kept to herself. She had put her heart and soul into what appeared to be a perfect part for her in a most distinguished play. That it was being so appallingly received in Edinburgh was incomprehensible to her.

Peter Brook and Christopher Fry arrived. Christopher Fry looked exhausted and straight away sat down, facing us. Peter Brook remained standing and gave us his prepared speech. 'Ladies and gentlemen,' he said, 'this is a council of war. For five weeks we have worked on Christopher's play. We have wrestled with its meaning, and tried to bring out its subtleties. We all thought it a beautiful play and we have done our best with it. But we have a flop on our hands. So now the tables are turned. Whereas in rehearsal we did what we could to serve Christopher, he has now agreed to serve us. So everything we want changed, Christopher will change. We have a long tour ahead of us so there is plenty of time for work: I envisage we shall rehearse most days.'

I asked about the snow, but was informed that that would not be changed. However, without a word to any of us, it was changed a fortnight later. Tiny pieces of white paper flickered prettily down outside the window. There were no more coughs. But it was too late to prevent the play from being ripped apart. It was felt that the plot was too thin, so new bits of story were added, while some of the more graceful arabesques of Christopher Fry's writing were cut. We became a most unhappy company, with Peter Brook hammering away at us, attempting, I'm sure, to make us better but driving us instead to despair. New words were up for grabs and the greedy actors bagged most of them, while the others found their parts being whittled away. John Moffatt's almost disappeared. The play became such a muddle that it was decided to publish it before the opening night in London, so the critics could read it in advance of seeing it and thereby hopefully understand what we were all talking about. Christopher Fry, depressed beyond measure, seemed to lose all control over it, and I had to dictate one of my new speeches, punctuation and all, to his secretary over the telephone while she was compiling the book.

The only thing that made the tour at all bearable for me was my growing friendship with Frances Hyland and David Spenser, and it was David who reminded me the other day that I was often ill with depression during the run of the play. I had forgotten that at one performance I was so sick that there had to be buckets in the wings by each of the exits so that I could quickly leave the stage to vomit when it wasn't my turn to speak. He said I was usually perfectly all right until I got to the theatre and was immediately well again when I left.

Half-way through the tour Frances was sacked. Her perform-ance was regarded as too mousey and insignificant, but she had been helped neither by the direction nor by the mouse-brown dress which had been designed for her. Margaret Johnston, in a black and white dress, replaced her and because she was more able to stand up for herself, contributed a lot to the play. But the alterations of moves and dialogue made for her by Peter Brook upset Dame Edith, and there were some nasty rows. Oh hell, I thought. Is it always going to be like this? Acting should be such a pleasure, and it is dreadful that it is such a pain. And when there are tantrums and unpleasantness, and when confidence gets knocked flat, what is the point of going on?

So I resolved to give up. I had had enough. I was getting nowhere so I might as well get out now and do something else. I would see the run of this play through, because I was contractually bound to do so, but as soon as it was over I would try for other work. I had an advertisement ready in my mind for the personal column of *The Times*: 'Young actor, tired of the stage, seeks other employment.'

It was never placed, and I did not give up. But the resolve to do so helped a bit. I didn't care any more, and as a consequence enjoyed the six-month run in London more than I thought I would.

Drama School Again

'Of all the jobs I have ever had, teaching at RADA is the one I should least like to have missed.' I am fond of saying that, and often mention it during interviews. I could go further and say, 'Teaching at RADA is the most important work I have ever done.' Important to me, that is, for it changed my life: it revived my confidence and warmed me up all over again. Suddenly to be thrust into the company of hordes of talented young people brimming with energy and expectation handed me back an excitement I had almost forgotten existed.

I loved the company of drama students and still do, although I rarely teach nowadays. They are unchanging in their keenness, their anxiety to please, their politeness and incredible charm. Sometimes I think they are the most beautiful people in the world, because they know what they are up against and, in spite of all the odds and all the warnings about the high rate of unemployment and the risks involved, they have recklessly dedicated themselves to the two or three years at RADA, or LAMDA, or the Guildhall or wherever, knowing that nothing may come of it but hoping against hope that something will. During their time there they will be exposed to a great deal of criticism, but they will be expected to put a brave face on it and to realize it is for their own good to persevere with improving their voices, their movement, their powers of observation, their interpretative ability and emotional range; and all the time they will be on show, stared at, worried over. They will become extremely conscious of their appearance, and start to look after themselves, because they will be told that their looks and the shape of their bodies are part and parcel of what they have to offer. Acting is, after all, putting one's whole self on show. One is naked, really, displaying all one's values and experiences and thoughts and emotions. It takes a lot of courage and a lot of love.

I admired many of the students and learned a lot from them. Diana Rigg, John Hurt, John Alderton, Caroline Blakiston, Susannah York, Sarah Miles, Edward Fox, Anthony Hopkins, Sarah Badel, Simon Ward, Ian Ogilvy; the writers Hugh Whitemore, David Pinner, Tom Kempinski and David Halliwell; Charles Kay, David Burke, Jennifer Hilary, Bridget Turner, Terence Rigby, David Warner, Siân Phillips, Roy Marsden, Susan Fleetwood, Robin Ray, Edward de Souza, Tom Courtenay, Bryan Marshall, Estelle Kohler, John Thaw, Geoffrey Hutchings, Gemma Jones, Bernard Lloyd, Peter Blythe, Sheila Gish, Rodney Bewes, Polly Adams, Ian McShane. These are just some of the people who have gone on to be successful performers; there are others who eventually became agents, directors or politicians, or who returned to their native America or Iceland or Israel; and there are many who are still struggling to get some sort of recognition, and a large, too large, number who never got anywhere at all, and have had to opt for other things.

In my book *About Acting* I described how it was that I came to be teaching at RADA. I applied for the job out of desperation, in an effort to prevent myself from going further downhill. I was twenty-six when I started to teach and some of the students were older than I was, but they called me Mr Barkworth, and I liked that; my classes were called Technique and I liked that too: it is a vague word and I used it to cover all the aspects of the art and craft of acting that I could think of. The first subject with every new group of students was always spontaneity. I would talk about it with them for the allotted two hours and at the end of it set an exercise which they were to perform the following week. The next subject, which I would deal with similarly, was speech and its varieties, the next, movement and gesture, then props, doings (laughing, crying, listening, drinking, kissing, etc.), comedy, pace, and so on and so on. I used improvisation a lot.

My new job enabled me to talk my heart out to an audience of acute and sometimes argumentative listeners. Nothing would escape them. They would stamp on anything woolly or inconsistent. I had to be clear; and I had to be entertaining, too: the worst sin of all for a teacher is to be boring. What I was really doing, though I didn't know it at the time, was clearing my mind of all the unnecessary thoughts, harmful superstitions, that had accumulated there over the years. At last I had something to do which forced me to concentrate not upon myself but upon other people. An actor is responsible for his own performance and that's that; a teacher is concerned with his students. When Athene Seyler had told me to 'think of the other people' I had found it difficult to do. Now I couldn't help but do it.

'I feel a bit like a doctor,' I said, as one student after another got up to do an exercise. 'I have to absorb everything I can while I'm watching you, and think what I want to say to you, and then try to say it well and helpfully: I have to concentrate totally on you. When I go to my doctor I expect him to listen to my story and think of the best remedy he can. But I know that when I have walked out of his surgery and closed the door he won't give me another thought. He mustn't, if he is going to give his next patient the attention he also will be expecting.'

So it was at RADA that I learned to concentrate: it absorbed me and made me fall in love again with the whole business of being an actor. I knew that in the students' eyes I had a head-start over many of the rest of the staff: I was a practising actor and not just a teacher, and they liked that and trusted me, and took me into their confidence. Not all of them, by any means. But enough to make the job seem special. I was one of them and we talked the same language. We had secret jargon words which nobody else knew about. I welcomed the curiously close, albeit vocational, relationships which sprang up with many of the students, and which have in some cases continued through the years and developed into friendships. John Hurt I often thought was the best student I ever encountered. One day recently I told him that. He said, 'Oh, but it was so easy. I just sussed out the sort of things you liked and the sort of things you didn't and did the things you liked and avoided the things you didn't. I mean, I knew what a huge emphasis you put on spontaneity in acting so I always tried to be as spontaneous as possible. I knew you liked total naturalness so I always tried to be as natural as possible. And when you told me about technical aids, well I just did them. For you. Just to please you. I don't know why all the others didn't do the same. It was easy.'

I think Robin Ray tried the same tactic and I was pleased when he took over my classes after I left in 1963. I remember being particularly fond of the class Robin was in, and they used to invite me occasionally to their parties. At one of these, in a sumptuous flat in Suffolk Street which three of the girls shared, I was horrified to find when I arrived, late from the theatre I was acting at, that they were in the middle of a most intense version of the truth game. (Anybody can ask anybody else any question they like and the answer *has* to be the unvarnished truth, otherwise you pay a forfeit and that can be much worse.) Of course I became the target for everybody's questions and Robin's were as sharp and surreptitious as anybody's. 'Who is your favourite student in our class?' and 'What do you think of the other teachers?' and 'Are you happy?' Eventually the game got out of hand and wouldn't

leave the subject of sex so we decided unanimously to abandon it
and to lie on the floor, separately, and listen to Rachmaninov's
2nd piano concerto and cool down a bit. It was extraordinary:
everybody listened, nobody talked. It was the best party I have
ever been to.

Only twice did I ever suggest to a student that he should give up
the idea of being an actor. It was a difficult thing to do and I hated
doing it. I am relieved that both of them have remained friends,
one especially, Hugh Whitemore, who has become such a
distinguished playwright.

Most of the students liked to see the plays I was in, and come
round afterwards and go for a drink and discuss my performance. I
liked it too, for my courage was rising. Even when I was off-form
and their reactions were damp I did not mind too much. 'It's all
part of it,' I would say, 'one can't be at one's best all the time. It's a
nuisance, but it's the same for everyone.' They would go away,
comforted; and I would walk home, warm as toast, to my little
attic flat in Bloomsbury, where I would eat a late supper and work
on the classes for the following day.

RADA was only five minutes' walk away. It contains the most
evocative smells of any building I know. There's a small stone
staircase down to the little theatre in the basement, and as you
descend it there are whiffs of greasepaint and powder from the
make-up room, of musty old clothes from the wardrobe, of
cigarette smoke from the countless fags smoked quickly in the
corridors during intervals, and finally, as you enter the theatre, of
canvas and wood and paint from the stage.

The larger theatre, the Vanbrugh, has a clean smell, like
Wright's coal tar. But the classrooms reek of stale breath and the
wood of old tables and chairs. The windows have to be shut
because of the deafening traffic in Gower Street, so the smells
have no escape except into the staircase and landings. The
canteen at the top smells perpetually of shepherd's pie.

I talk about RADA because it is the only drama school I know. I have friends who studied at LAMDA, the Webber-Douglas, the Guildhall, the Central and the Bristol Old Vic, who speak equally warmly about their drama schools. They are happy places on the whole, though they have their detractors: students who have previously been to a university often find them childish and rather silly. And of course the merit of each drama school is determined by the standard of talent of the teachers and directors it employs, a standard which is ominously variable. Some students, landed with too many teachers of questionable ability, are just unlucky.

But the schools I have listed deserve their reputation and continue to flourish. What is there to choose between them? My preference is for those which offer the shortest courses. I have always thought that two years is enough. If you can't prepare a student to be ready for the profession in two years, then something is wrong with either the student or the school. It may feel a bit rushed but that is all to the good. It's all right to be breathless. Three years is too safe, in my view. The profession is hard, nervous and vibrant, and to protect the students and wrap them in cotton-wool for three years will not prepare them for its dangers. Besides, young actors have their youth to offer and should be out and about as soon as possible.

I would also choose a London school. London is where you will find all the casting directors, agents, television people, film people, radio people and theatre people you could wish for to give you a leg start and help you on your way. They are often invited for special events, and most of them are only too keen to attend. Competition to snap up the best, or perhaps the showiest, students can be surprisingly fierce, and hard on those to whom no offers are made. But that's as it is in the profession, too, and we have to get used to it. 'My turn will come,' we have all said, over and over and over.

The curriculum varies considerably from school to school. I am always surprised that Technique is seldom included as a subject, for it encapsulates so much of that part of acting which can be taught; but I like the growing practice, in some schools but not all, of working in front of cameras, both film and television. There are many secrets to be learned, and it is ridiculous to withhold them. 'Where would we be without television?' we often say, for it is where many of us do most of our work. Too much concentration on theatre is misleading.

One evening recently I revisited RADA, my favourite among my first houses, to watch advanced students perform audition speeches. I was one of three adjudicators, and we sat behind a table in the darkened stalls, writing our notes under Anglepoise lamps as each student went through his or her solitary paces. Several members of staff were there, dotted about near us, blank-faced and anxious. The students were allowed to sit in the circle, and they egged their classmates on with roars of laughter at the slightest jokes, and cheers and whistles and stamping of feet at the end of each piece. It was like a football match, or *Jeux Sans Frontières*.

At the end of it all, towards midnight, we delivered our solemn-sounding verdicts, and although we agreed that some were good and some were bad, our opinions as to which were good and which were bad were embarrassingly at variance. We agreed, however, that audition speeches need an enormous amount of care in preparation: the choice should be apt, the character studied as though for the play, and the staging controlled but adventurous. 'The trouble with auditions,' I said, 'is that you have to make an impression so quickly. The people who are watching you will make up their minds about you in two minutes flat, as we have done tonight. It's instant-decision time. And the trouble with instant decisions is that they stick. It's very unsatisfactory and a lot of directors and casting directors don't choose from auditions any more, but a lot still do and it's something we have to live with.'

It is as well, when auditioning to get into a drama school, to have professional coaching. The competition is appallingly fierce. In September 1979 306 boys and 444 girls auditioned for RADA. Fifteen boys and eight girls were accepted. In September 1981 357 boys and 544 girls tried. Fifteen boys and eight girls were accepted.

It's a tough world.

Peter Sallis as the First Gravedigger, me as the Second, in Hamlet at the Sheffield Playhouse.

With Clive Brook in A Woman of No Importance.

Athene Seyler, seated, surrounded by Aubrey Mather, me, Nora Swinburne and Frances Hyland.

With Margaret Johnston in The Dark is Light Enough.

The original cast of Roar Like a Dove, with *Anne Kimbell holding the baby, surrounded by Evelyn Varden, John McCallum, Ewan Roberts, Waveney Lee, Anthony Ireland and (kneeling) Paul McGrath, with me as the outcast.*

(Anthony Buckley & Constantine Ltd)

Just managing a shy smile at the photo-call.
(Anthony Buckley & Constantine Ltd)

My confidence was growing.

Success

And just as the sap in me was rising I was offered a part in Lesley Storm's new play, *Roar Like A Dove*.

I knew as soon as I read it that it was the best part I had had in London so far: Bernard Taggart-Stewart, a sensitive young man from London, out of his depth and miserable on a large estate in the Western Highlands of Scotland where, as he said, there were 'cows having calves, horses having foals, hundreds of shivering little lambs popping out on those freezing hillsides – dogs having pups in the barns, cats having kittens in the lofts! My God it's a nightmare!' This squeamish, nervous fellow had only one scene, at the beginning of the second act. After it he escaped from 'all this sickening fertility' and went back to London. But it was a gift: for fifteen glorious minutes he was the central character in one of the funniest passages in the play.

The cast was happily chosen, led by John McCallum and three spendid Americans: Anne Kimbell, Paul McGrath and Evelyn Varden. The director was Murray Macdonald, a punctilious Scot with smooth black hair and a low threshold of boredom. He directed us like a dream, wafting us around the stage with perfectly conceived moves, encouraging us to be as light and sparkling as possible. He was precise but never dictatorial, and we all felt free to do what we wanted. 'Do as you please as long as it's good' was his motto. But he was a superb technician and gave me lots of tips, especially about comedy:

'Peter. I've placed you deliberately on the other side of the stage from the little girl, so that the audience will have to look either at her or at you. They will not be able to look at you both at the same time. It's odd to do this in a comedy, but I've done it because we can't expect the little girl to keep still during your funny lines and if the audience could see you both in the same eyeful I think she might be distracting. This does mean, however, that you'll have to make them look at you just before you speak. *Just* before. You'll have to be clever and think of different little movements to attract their attention: you can put your hand through your hair, or raise a finger towards her or something. Lots of things. Leave it to you.

'Peter: if you cross your legs on that line you'll get a louder laugh. I don't know why but you will.

'Peter: when you walk away from somebody try to walk not in a straight line but in an arc. And when you turn back to them, complete the circle of the arc. Do you understand? Turn in the direction you've already established by the arc. That's right. Looks better.

'Peter: when you are nervous, underplay. Good actors tend to overact when they are nervous.

'Peter: don't tell us all about the part the minute you come on, otherwise you'll have nowhere to go. The audience should be surprised by you from time to time. It'll be funnier. A performance should mount, not diminish. So come on gently, and try and arrange it so that your loudest laugh will be your last. It's not good to get loud laughs straight away. Edith told me that, and she's right.'

Murray was another director who handed out help and love in equal proportions. He had a delightful knack of apparently taking everyone into his confidence: he made us all feel, separately, that we were his special favourite, on whom he relied for comfort.

I was sitting in the stalls, watching a rehearsal one day, and Murray was pacing about restlessly. Occasionally he would come up to me and whisper waspish asides about the actors. One of them had not done enough homework and was struggling away with the lines and getting prompt after prompt. 'Look at him!' whispered Murray. 'Look at the fool! Why doesn't he do some work? I get so bored when actors don't know the lines I sometimes want to give up directing altogether.' Another actor wasn't doing a telephone conversation very well. 'Well I'm not going to tell him how to do it,' the whispering continued, 'he must work it out for himself. He knows it's not good. If he can't do it on his own he ought not to be on the stage.' And he lit yet another cigarette and paced all over the stalls.

'You must make it your own' was one of his favourite sayings. At the end of a rehearsal one day he gave me a new piece of business to try out, and showed me how to do it. It was a special way of holding the little girl's doll by the legs and throwing it aside. Then he said, 'Don't do it now, because all you'll do is copy me. Make it your own, and do it tomorrow at the run-through.' I couldn't think of any other way of doing it so I did just as he had demonstrated. When he was giving notes after the run-through he said, 'Oh yes, Peter, good, that new idea of yours with the doll, holding it by the legs like that. Good. Yes.'

Armed with the confidence such a director inspires, we opened full of expectation in Leeds on 2 September 1957. During the performance Murray paced about back-stage and in the corridors adjoining the auditorium, chain-smoking. He was too nervous to watch, he said, but he listened to every word and to every laugh. The play went wonderfully well, but it lasted three hours and everybody agreed that it needed cutting. 'Not your part,' Murray whispered, 'not a word of your part.' And he looked so warm and pleased with me. Then he said, seriously, 'All you need to do now, during the three-week tour, is close up the gaps. Let your only pauses be those while the audience is laughing. Try and get rid of all the others. Then your performance will be perfect.'

A glorious First Night in London at the Phoenix Theatre was followed by a sufficient number of ecstatic reviews to ensure our success. And for the first time I received glowing mentions from many of the critics. 'The whole of London is talking about you,' said Murray, with a glint in his eye. I was on cloud nine and didn't come down for a very long time.

The play ran for nearly three years. There were many changes of cast – over ten little girls came and went (on account of their breasts growing too big for the part) – but Ewan Roberts and I stayed the course. This time I didn't mind the long run at all, because my days were full to overflowing. There was my flat to look after, and RADA to go to, and private lessons to give (a guinea for an hour or ten and sixpence for half); and I was given quite a lot of work by a friend who produced a weekly television programme. Murray Macdonald employed me, too, as his assistant director for *Marigold*, a musical at the Savoy and later the Saville, and *The Amorous Prawn* which had a long and successful run at the Saville and later the Piccadilly. He also asked me to 'look after' *Roar Like A Dove*, rehearsing some of the cast changes. 'You do it,' he said peevishly, 'I can't listen to it any more.'

It was a welter of work. Whenever I could I escaped on Sundays into the countryside to go for long walks on my own, so that I could have a bit of peace and quiet, and time for a think. Sevenoaks to Tonbridge, the South Downs near Arundel, the far side of the Isle of Wight and the borders of Sussex and Kent. I still find it easier to think things out while walking in the open air than when cooped up in a room. My diaries, which I had started to write again, often complain of tiredness, and no wonder. But they are full of the delight I felt for everything I had to do:

Tuesday 17 March 1959

Tonight as I walked back from the theatre I thought I caught a glimpse of my morning-self, hurrying to RADA along the north side of Russell Square, and disappearing through the arch of Senate House – which tonight was floodlit. I love this little flat, so near the centre of things, so typical of Bloomsbury with its cosmopolitan studiousness and its mixture of the bookish and the carefree. Here I feel so far away and yet so near. This morning at the RADA I watched an hour of Upper Middle 2A's Shakespeare test, unremarkable except for Edward Fox who is very remarkable, very talented and very odd. A nice two-hour period with Middle A, and lunch in the canteen. Down to the Halifax Building Society to pay in cheques, up to the dentist in Belsize Park, back to RADA to see part of *Heartbreak House*, home for tea and a lesson to Tracy Reed, and to the theatre for a good performance.

The BBC decided they would like to do a live television excerpt from *Roar Like A Dove* with an invited audience. It was to last half an hour and they wanted it to start with the end of Act I, which was Evelyn Varden's best bit, and end with my scene. Of course the rest of the play would be played as usual. Murray was pleased with their choice and thought it would be good for business, which had been falling off slightly. We were all very excited about the idea, and practised doing our parts with no facial expression whatsoever because we thought that would be best for all the close-ups we were bound to receive. We realized we'd still have to speak up, though, because we would want the laughs from the invited audience.

Who are they going to invite, we wondered? I was horrified when I heard the answer. The whole of RADA was to occupy the upper circle. 'Oh no,' I said, 'not them! It'll be more frightening doing it in front of them than in front of the television cameras. Oh can't it be changed?' I pleaded.

'No,' was the answer.

All day we rehearsed, and we were given one or two new moves to make it easier for the cameras. We rehearsed these changes over and over again so that we would remember them and do them well.

I was dreadfully nervous as I waited to do my scene. Evelyn Varden went down very well and got a lot of applause, and I thought I would be a terrible let-down after that. But I had forgotten the generosity of drama students, especially one's own, and from my very first line they roared with laughter. Roared like a dove, indeed! They led the audience for the entire scene, and when it came finally to my exit they cheered me to the echo, and I knew those cheers would be heard through the length and breadth of the nation. Telegrams of congratulation arrived later in the evening, the whole of RADA came back-stage, and the following morning there were some more ecstatic reviews. This time in the television columns.

So with the coming together of the play I was to live with for so long, the drama school I loved so much, and television – which was to occupy me so completely in years to come – my cup, for the moment, was full.

Coda

There is scant mention in this book of what is, for many actors, the most difficult hurdle of all to overcome: a prolonged period of unemployment. We all expect gaps between engagements, but when weeks become months and months become years without a single worthwhile offer, the resulting depression can know no bounds. When there's nothing to do there is too much time to brood; the ever-present questions remain unanswered: '*Why* does no one want me? What is it about *me* that puts people off?'

I had one such period in 1964. I waited for the telephone to ring, and I had to go on waiting for seven months. I had stopped teaching at RADA, so there was nothing to disguise the fact that I was completely and utterly out of work. Twice a week, every Monday and Wednesday, I traipsed across Hampstead Heath and down through Kentish Town to the labour exchange in Camden Town, where they got to know me well. After a few months I thought I would never work again, and became ill with depression. 'I feel as low as the bottom of the sea,' I wrote in my diary.

Many of my friends have had similar times, and I am always astonished at the brave face they put on it, at their resilience and undying hope. The worst is when people say, 'What are you doing now?' and you have to say, 'Nothing.' It sounds so complete, that

'Nothing.' Even now, when I am between jobs, sometimes for quite a long time, I hate saying 'Nothing.' I want to excuse it, and talk about future possibilities, or, if I know what I am going to do next, talk about that, or about what I have just done. I try to resist the temptation, but I wish they hadn't asked: sometimes I have a sneaking suspicion that one or two of them will be *glad* to hear 'Nothing', and will smile secretly about it when they get home.

There are positive things that can be done during out-of-work periods to help relieve the monotony and strain. Audition speeches can be worked on and job-letters written. If there's a little cash available there are excellent classes – now called talk-ins or workshops or seminars or masterclasses – at the Actors' Centre and the City Lit., as there are, too, at the major drama schools.

They help a little, these things. Might as well use the time profitably. Usually they will seem to be no more than occupational therapy, however, for it's so easy to be apathetic and develop a don't-care-about-anything attitude. Days drag. Washing-up can take an hour, and then it's time for a lie-down.

I have said it before: it's hard to call yourself an actor when you are not acting. And I am proud to call myself an actor, although, like most of us, I have a love-hate relationship with it all. I look forward to performing but it's always with a certain amount of dread. And indeed it is a life full of contradictions: it is truly insecure and yet it is exciting; it demands total dedication and a huge capacity for work, and yet it appears glamorous and carefree; a long run in the theatre can become tedious and boring, while a play for radio is over before you know how to do it; there's not enough work to go round, and yet it always seems to be the same people who get it, and they are the ones, too, who do all those extra things like playing panel games on television, or being interviewed by Michael Parkinson, or recording commentaries for films and voice-overs for commercials; and they get free meals at the Savoy at award ceremonies and lots of gifts and presentations; but they give a lot, too, of their time and their money, and are bombarded by charities. We are a feudal society: there are the rich and there are the poor, though it's not as bad as it used to be and it will get better still. Theatre, like the political world, has gradually turned towards the left, and has benefited from the turn.

And in spite of the contradictions there is the strongest of bonds which unites us: we talk the same language and know what's going on. There is a quite extraordinary friendliness between us, and when we meet up again with somebody we worked with years ago, it's as though it were only yesterday that we last saw them. There is no group of people more generous, gossipy, warm-hearted, self-obsessed, affectionate, critical, entertaining, high-spirited and giving than actors and actresses, and I, for one, am glad to be in their ranks, though sometimes it seems like a madness.

Index